Predictions
for the
Next Millennium

Predictions for the Next Millennium

Thoughts on the 1,000 Years Ahead from Today's Celebrities

David Kristof and Todd W. Nickerson

**Andrews McMeel
Publishing**

Kansas City

98 99 00 01 RDC 10 9 8 7 6 5 4 3 2

www.andrewsmcmeel.com

Library of Congress Cataloging-in-Publication Data

Kristof, David.
    Predictions for the next millennium : thoughts on the 1,000 years
    ahead from celebrities of today / David Kristof and Todd W. Nickerson.
        p.   cm.
    Includes index.
    ISBN 0-8362-6916-0 (hd)
    1. Twenty-first century—Forecasts—Quotations, maxims, etc.
    2. Celebrities—Quotations. I. Nickerson, Todd W. II. Title.
    CB161.K74 1998
    303.49'0905—dc21   98-7513
                                                            CIP

To Nora Kristof and Josephine "Dee Dee" Bostrom,
who did not live to see the next millennium
but will never be forgotten.

———————————

To my wife Lisa,
and sons Sam and Noah

Contents

Acknowledgments

As the founders of the Millennium Committee of New York, LLC, we have been overwhelmed with the success of this project. It is nearly impossible to separate those to be thanked for the creation of this book from those to be thanked for their assistance to the overall project. However, our first and foremost appreciation must be extended to each and every one of the celebrities who has contributed a message to our endeavor.

These prominent people were obviously in no way obligated to respond to our requests—and many of their peers did in fact ignore or decline the opportunity to provide millennial predictions. That the names on the following pages (and hundreds more) did see value in investing part of their time to create these messages reveals their genuine interest in the direction of our world. We think their ideas are spectacular, and we thank them profoundly for their consideration.

In addition to these contributors, numerous other people must also be thanked—both for the project's success and for the book's completion.

The fact that Lisa Nickerson remains happily married to one of this book's authors is a testimonial of her love, support, and patience. Lisa, and sons Sam and Noah, endured Daddy's work schedule for more than a year in which nearly every spare moment was spent hunched over a glowing computer screen or preparing mailings. The fact that this book's other author remains every bit the bachelor he began the process as is a testimonial to the nonexistent social life that is the trademark of any good book project.

Books are not published on merit and hard work alone, and for this book's publication we must thank Karen Gantz Zahler for her efforts. She believed in this project's viability from our first cautious meeting at New York's "21" Club. Both a literary agent and attorney, Karen has amazed us from the start by her ability to succesfully hold two of the most challenging occupations in society and yet still be a truly nice person.

It was our later good fortune to encounter an extraordinary publicist in Cathy Saypol. Whether it has been e-mailing us from her other office in Hawaii or chasing down people on Capitol Hill, Cathy has generously given her talents to this book's success.

We also thank our attorney friends, Doug Arpert

and Alan Hock, whose energy, judgment, and counsel helped contribute to our early confidence and direction. For business advice, Professors Dick Ottoway and Leo Rogers of Fairleigh Dickinson University's business program proved to be valuable sounding boards at a time when we may have appeared to be quite unsound. And for his many hours of time and advice on the television industry, we must thank Steve Thomas of WGBH's *This Old House*.

Special thanks go to Donna Kristof, whose frequent willingness to stamp hundreds of envelopes until 3 A.M. makes her not only a great office worker but a greater sister. Special thanks also to Phyllis and Rev. Carl Kearns and David and Edith Nickerson, whose consistently wise advice and encouragement from the beginning provided crucial guidance when needed most.

As our exhibition began as a New York endeavor, we would be remiss for not thanking Ann Godfrey of the N.Y. Visitors Bureau for her advice, as well as Mayor Rudolph Giuliani, who is making New York a great city once again. Lee Kessler of the White House Millennium Council also provided us with key advice. Lydia Ruth and Stephen Tole at the Empire State Building and Bruce Morrow at WBCS have also been most helpful to our cause.

Further thanks go to Yuri Bokanev, John Briod, Ralph Fylstra, Jim Hyde, Martin and Eileen Kristof, Bryan McGuire, Dennis Oliver, Richard Rubenstein, Bob Smolinsky, Rick Sondik, Christabel Vartanian, Mitch Werner, and Alexander Yui, all of whom have provided valuable input along the way. For our operational success, we acknowledge the many postal workers of the United Nations, who patiently accepted and sorted crate after crate of our mailings. Thanks to Larry Lattera and Larry Schwartz for photographic support and Carlos Graziano for his many foreign language translations. And many thanks to our terrific editor, Kathy Viele of Andrews McMeel, who patiently tolerated us over the past several months and without whom this book could not have been a success.

We must also thank our many friends at Lucent Technologies, the company we have worked at for our entire professional lives and a company we believe will deliver many of the next millennium's great innovations.

Finally, we wish to extend our deepest respects to the families of nine contributors to this project: Dr. Christian Anfinsen, Eddie Arcaro, Sir Derek H. R. Barton, Samuel Fuller, Phil Hartman, Burgess Meredith, James Michener, Buffalo Bob Smith, and Dr. Benjamin Spock. These men did not live to see the new millennium, but the spirit of their ideas will always be with us.

Introduction

As we stand at the twilight of what have surely been the most astounding century and millennium of mankind, the vast potential of the next millennium lies before us. We will not live to see most of it, and so we are resigned to enjoy its unknown wonders only through our own imaginations. This book provides more than 250 imagined futures—predictions for the next millennium—from some of the most accomplished persons of our time.

Our era is defined by such people. Their music inspires us, their medicine cures us, their art strikes us, their leadership governs us, their drama moves us, their discoveries evolve us, their humor amuses us, and their writings engross us. Although their predictive powers may be no better than any randomly chosen group, their successful grasp of today's realities makes their visions of the future perhaps the most alluring.

Predictions are not a science, of course, and no amount of intellectual or artistic genius can ever assure the certainty of a future event. Perhaps the value of a prediction is in its creativity, not its accuracy. Despite the occasionally uncanny foresight of Leonardo da Vinci or Jules Verne, these and other wise people made numerous predictions that appear comical today. As historian Pierre Berton pointed out to us, H. G. Wells once predicted—circa 1900—that the next world war would be fought on bicycles.

Whether this book will provide great amusement to the readers of the year 3000 we cannot say. For today's readers, however, we hope this book will add meaning to their turn-of-the-millennium experience. This milestone in time is truly a rare occasion—we will become the first generation of mankind to universally observe the passing of a millennium. Whether it prompts celebration or introspection, this is an event that will be remembered. Time zone by time zone, we will all pass into a new age, never again to exist in the Second Millennium. . . . What will the next millennium bring?

As the founders of the Millennium Committee of New York, LLC, we began asking this question in 1996. We concluded that a museum-quality exhibition of written predictions would commemorate the event and serve as a meaningful time capsule. We also believed that the public would be most interested in messages from celebrities, with our definition of "celebrity" including scientists, Nobel laureates, foreign dignitaries, and other accomplished individuals who have had a profound impact on today's world. Over the following months, we began correspondences, and even friendships, with an amazing number of such people.

Despite being inexperienced in the world of public relations and celebrities, we soon learned that the merits of the idea enabled us to have many personally rewarding encounters. From an engaging dinner with Fred Goldman, to discussing the moon's landscape with astronaut Harrison Schmitt, to a millennial debate with Arthur C. Clarke, this project has been a gratifying and fascinating experience.

We asked contributors to describe an event that they predict—or hope—will occur between the years 2001 and 3000. The subject matter, disposition, and length of each prediction were left entirely to each contributor. The result was a collection of ideas and a list of contributors as diverse as the world itself, incorporating not only every area of accomplishment but also every continent on the planet (with over seventy nations represented).

Each contributor was asked to write his or her message on the back of a postcard we purchased from the bookstore of the United Nations. Each celebrity received a postcard bearing the flag of his or her native country. The following pages feature selections from some of the hundreds of responses that our organization has received. In addition to the prediction and a brief biography, we have provided each contributor's birthplace and their "Age at the Millennium" (that person's age as of January 1, 2001—the scientifically correct start date of the Third Millennium that we have grown to respect over January 1, 2000).

The messages in this book are reproduced in their original form. It should be noted that the Millennium Committee of New York, LLC, is a privately funded organization not affiliated with any political or religious body, including the city of New York or the United Nations. Striving to create an objective and unbiased project, we have made no attempt to edit, manipulate, or provide commentary on any of the ideas expressed within this book. However, we do believe that the concepts of democracy and freedom that the U. S. Constitution guarantees, coupled with the goal of world peace declared by the United Nations, are worthy charters for the world to embrace in the new millennium.

Our relatively simple project has delivered a surprising number of opportunities to test our philosophy. For example, our communications with the People's Republic of China resulted in us having to decline their request that we exclude the Dalai Lama and all other Taiwanese or Tibetan contributors, resulting in the non-participation of China's political leaders. On the other hand, our visit to the Russian consulate in New York to discuss this project in detail was an uplifting experience that demonstrated how former political adversaries can truly cooperate.

If there is a pattern to these millennial messages, it is that we are clearly at a crossroads. Many celebrities speak eloquently of the marvels that await mankind in the future, yet a great many others express concern over the consequences of the technological and social patterns that have characterized our recent past. Human morality, population growth, law and order, war and peace, technology, and the environment all provide weighty dilemmas for the future.

For all our modern enlightenment, however, it is ironic that our turn-of-the-millennium generation has brought the world close to the realities of environmental and nuclear destruction. Yet, we have fared well so far, and if the following pages are any indication, we clearly possess the wisdom to find the answers for future generations.

We are in awe of past legacies, yet we cannot know what our descendants will find awesome in us. We can hope, however, that the following messages will prove to our descendants that we truly had their fates in mind. And as we say good-bye to what has been the most amazing millennium in human history, we can only imagine the time that lies ahead.

We encourage readers interested in this millennium project to attend its exhibition between 1999 and 2001. The original documents are quite impressive to view in person. The collection includes hundreds of additional predictions that are not featured in this book. Information regarding the exhibition can be found at our Internet site, www.2001-3000.com. This site provides up-to-date details of where and when the exhibition will be shown, a complete list of the project's contributors, and links to other related Internet sites.

Following the exhibition, we hope the cards will survive the millennium and periodically be redisplayed for the fascination of subsequent generations—our increasingly distant descendants.

Chapter 1

Television and Film

OLIVER STONE

Birthplace:
New York, N.Y.

**Age at the
Millennium:** 54

One of the most powerful directors in
Hollywood, Oliver Stone has gained a reputation
for carefully detailed films that are both
controversial and hugely successful. His movies
include *Platoon, JFK, Natural Born Killers*, and
Nixon.

United Nations   Nations Unies
NEW YORK   GENÈVE

DNA will evolve to the next state – with or without
the present world population. Mind culture – and
artificial intelligence – will replace word culture.

Oliver Stone

Santa Monica, California   1997

UNITED
NATIONS

A popular television, film, and Broadway actor, Judd Hirsch twice received the Best Comedy Actor Emmy Award for the television series *Taxi*. He has since done other sitcoms, several movies, and won two Tony Awards.

Birthplace:
New York, N.Y.

Age at the Millennium: 65

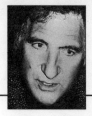

JUDD HIRSCH

United Nations   Nations Unies
NEW YORK   GENÈVE

— Judd Hirsch

IF THIS SPACE-AGE, THIS LATTER SECOND MILLENNIUM, HAS TAUGHT US ANYTHING, IT IS THAT WE LIVE ON A FRAGILE PLANET WITH AN ONION-SKIN ATMOSPHERE, CONTAINING ALL THAT IS DEAR TO NATURAL LIFE. AND THAT WE HUMANS ARE RAPIDLY TURNING ALL OF IT TO WASTE, INCLUDING EVEN THE NARROWEST BAND OF BREATHABLE AIR, AT AN ALARMING RATE OF POLLUTION, DESTRUCTION AND OVERPOPULATION. AND IF WE HAVE LEARNED ANYTHING SIGNIFICANT FROM THE FIRST TWO MILLENNIUMS, IT WOULD BE THAT WE ONLY HAVE A TINY FRACTION OF THE THIRD MILLENNIUM TO CHANGE IT. I ONLY WISH I COULD PREDICT WE SHALL !

Judd Hirsch
1997 - New York City

UNITED NATIONS

If this space-age, this latter second millennium, has taught us anything, it is that we live on a fragile planet with an onion-skin atmosphere, containing all that is dear to natural life. And that we humans are rapidly turning all of it to waste, including even the narrowest band of breathable air, at an alarming rate of pollution, destruction and overpopulation. And if we have learned anything significant from the first two millenniums, it would be that we only have a tiny fraction of the third millennium to change it. I only wish I could predict we shall!

NICHELLE NICHOLS

Birthplace:
Chicago, Ill.

Age at the Millennium: 62

Originally a teenage singer with Duke Ellington's band, Nichelle Nichols gained lasting fame when chosen by Gene Roddenberry to play the role Uhura in the experimental television series *Star Trek*. Nichols is also an accomplished author.

United Nations   Nations Unies
NEW YORK   GENÈVE

BY 2020: Fusion energy plants under construction around the world. Robotic "creatures," easily interpret voice commands, doing much of the labor humans have traditionally done. The Earth Drug Council is formed with multi-national power and financial means to eradicate illegal drug traffic.

BY 2050: The Earth, Environmental and Space Councils are formed, the latter with jurisdiction over Moon and Mars colonizations, Exploration of Europa and Titan underway. Continental based economic units formed, primarily to conduct international trade, practically erasing national boundaries within the geographic units.

BY 2350: STAR TREK re-runs still playing on TV. Crew of the starship Enterprise watch re-runs while they begin their first inter-galactic mission.

BY 3000: Earth's politicians are taking interplanetary economic lessons from alien beings in attempt to learn how to operate a government without taxing people to death. (Circa: late 20th century)

Ref: "SATURN'S CHILD" by Nichelle Nichols (G.P. Putnam's Sons - 1995)

UNITED NATIONS

- BY 2020: Fusion energy plants under construction around the world. Robotic "creatures," easily interpret voice commands, doing much of the labor humans have traditionally done. The Earth Drug Council is formed with multi-national power and financial means to eradicate illegal drug traffic.

- BY 2050: The Earth Environmental and Space Councils are formed, the latter with jurisdiction over Moon and Mars colonizations. Exploration of Europa and Titan underway. Continental based economic units formed, primarily to conduct international trade, practically erasing national boundaries within the geographic units.

- BY 2350: STAR TREK re-runs still playing on TV. Crew of the Starship Enterprise watch re-runs while they begin their first inter-galactic mission.

- BY 3000: Earth's politicians are taking interplanetary economic lessons from alien beings in attempt to learn how to operate a government without taxing people to death (Circa: late 20th century)

Ref: "Saturn's Child" by Nichelle Nichols (G.P. Putnam's Sons-1995)

5   A brilliant but controversial filmmaker, Leni Riefenstahl will best be remembered for the Third Reich film *Triumph of the Will,* which she presented to Adolf Hitler. Riefenstahl later denounced any political leanings and is now an acclaimed nature photographer.

**Birthplace:
Berlin, Germany**

**Age at the
Millennium: 98**

LENI RIEFENSTAHL

The changes in our world from today concerning the development of science and technology are so much speedy, that one can only suspect, what will happen to us in the future. This trend goes clearly away from nature, which will be destroyed more and more. Woods will disappear, oceans will be more dirty and fished empty.

In 1000 years there will be hardly a living space for people on this earth. Before the final destruction people will find other planets and will be able to make them habitable because of their genius technical abilities.

This is my vision.

Leni Riefenstahl
June 1997

Photo by Folkwang-Archiv

ANTHONY QUINN

**Birthplace:
Chihuahua, Mexico**

**Age at the
Millennium: 85**

A Hollywood legend, Anthony Quinn has won two Academy Awards and has been in more than 300 films since 1936, including *Viva Zapata* and *Zorba the Greek*. Quinn is also an accomplished painter.

United Nations   Nations Unies
NEW YORK   GENÈVE

WITH ALL THE NEW
IMPROVEMENTS, THE NEW
CENTURY MUST FIND ANSWERS
TO A COMMON CURRENCY, A
COMMON LANGUAGE AND A
COMMON POLITICAL
PHILOSOPHY. ALL THE

REST IS ICING ON

Address

THE CAKE.

©
UNITED
NATIONS

Photo by Express Newspapers /Archive Photos

One of the more famous alumni of *Saturday Night Live*, Phil Hartman also appeared in fourteen motion pictures. In 1996 he became the star of the highly acclaimed television sitcom *News Radio*. Mr. Hartman died in 1998 at the age of 49.

Birthplace: Brantford, Canada

Deceased 1998

PHIL HARTMAN

United Nations   Nations Unies
NEW YORK   GENÈVE

1/29/98

EARLY IN THE NEW MILLENIUM I WOULD LIKE TO SEE A HEALTHY KIND OF TEEN REBELLION. AND I PREDICT YOUNG PEOPLE IN TROUBLED PARTS OF THE WORLD LIKE ISRAEL, BOSNIA, AND NORTHERN IRELAND WILL REJECT THE TRADITIONS OF HATRED THAT ARE PASSED FROM ONE GENERATION TO THE NEXT. PEOPLE EVERYWHERE WILL SENSE OUR COMMON ORIGIN AND OUR COMMON DESTINY. THUS, MAY PEACE PREVAIL ON EARTH.

Address

PHIL HARTMAN
ENCINO, CALIFORNIA

UNITED NATIONS

Early in the new millennium I would like to see a healthy kind of teen rebellion. And I predict young people in troubled parts of the world like Israel, Bosnia, and Northern Ireland will reject the traditions of hatred that are passed from one generation to the next. People everywhere will sense our common origin and our common destiny. Thus, may peace prevail on Earth.

EDWARD ASNER

Birthplace:
Kansas City, Mo.

**Age at the
Millennium: 71**

One of television's strongest actors, Edward Asner's most famous role came in 1970 as the character Lou Grant. He has performed in numerous other television, film, and stage roles, and has received a total of seven Emmy Awards.

8

My prediction is that 2001-3000 will, after great amounts of all kinds of war, (local and major) usher in a world government that will heal the planet and preserve all life forms in addition to achieving a state where man's conscience is allowed to catch up with his brain.

Edward Asner

**Edward Asner
1997
Studio City, CA**

Joan Rivers's controversially blunt humor has made her a popular stand-up comedian since the 1960s. After numerous appearances on the *Johnny Carson Show,* Rivers began her own talk shows in 1986.

Birthplace:
New York, N.Y.

Age at the
Millennium: 67

JOAN RIVERS

United Nations   Nations Unies
NEW YORK   GENÈVE

My prediction is that in the new Millennium, interest rates will be higher and my breasts will be lower —

Joan Rivers
May 5, 1997
New York City

Address

©
UNITED
NATIONS

My prediction is that in the new millennium, interest rates will be higher and my breasts will be lower.

CHRISTOPHER LEE

Birthplace:
London, England

Age at the
Millennium: 78

An acclaimed British actor, Christopher Lee appeared in his first film in 1947. Lee is known for his flawless portrayal of villainous characters, starring in movies such as *Dracula, Man with the Golden Gun,* and *The Three Musketeers.*

United Nations   Nations Unies
NEW YORK   GENÈVE

Although it seems machines are taking over, I feel there will undoubtedly be great advances in the field of science and medicine, resulting in the possibility of creating life itself. I wish I believed that the world would be a better place, but such is the decline in human behaviour + morals over the last 50 years, mostly due to greed, that I fear for the future of civilisation in general + humanity in particular.

Christopher Lee
May '97

Address

London
England

© UNITED NATIONS

Although it seems machines are taking over, I feel there will undoubtedly be great advances in the field of science and medicine, resulting in the possibility of creating life itself. I wish I believed that the world would be a better place, but such is the decline in human behaviour and morals over the last 50 years, mostly due to greed, that I fear for the future of civilisation in general and humanity in particular.

One of the best-known actors in the world, Jackie Chan enjoys film success in both the East and West. Mixing martial arts, action, and comedy, Chan performs his own stunts and works without a budget.

Birthplace: Hong Kong

Age at the Millennium: 46

JACKIE CHAN

Because of filmmaking or participating in related activities, I have traveled to most of the corners of the world, and witnessed many places that were rich, prosperous and with beautiful landscapes turn into desolate, poor and backward countries. The answer for the cause of these changes is almost always war. Fights between tribes, battles between countries, wars between different religious beliefs.

No matter what kind of warfare, there is always a common objective, and that is the killing of people by other people. Even if wars finally end, the destruction and poverty left behind will torture the surviving people for decades to come. And just when people start rebuilding their homes from the ashes of war, old arguments will resurface again and cause new conflicts. Faced with the upcoming year 2000, I have a humble but wasteful wish, and that is for humanity not to wage war again. I say that the wish is humble and wasteful, because although everyone undoubtedly understands that wars bring disaster, every day there are still wars going on.

I also wish that without having to wait until the year 2000, starting right here from today, regardless if the dispute is for the distribution of resources and food between tribes, for land or ideology between countries, or even for the belief of different gods between religions, we can use our best efforts to avoid going the way of war, and instead, negotiate and resolve it in a calm, cool-headed rational manner.

The problem is that even as I say it myself, I feel that it is naïve and laughable. No wonder it is not easy to dissipate wars by using conventional wisdom. But we call ourselves the master of all things, and within the span of a few hundred years, starting from when Columbus held on to the idea that the world was round, and eventually discovered the new continent, to today's space walks, our knowledge has seen an immeasurable advancement because we were able to break away from the bias that any dispute ultimately has to be resolved by way of belligerent forces?

If we can break this bias, then the next millennium will be an era of advancement and progress unmatched before by humankind.

If humans have enough wisdom.

對快將來臨的 2000 年的期望

為了拍攝電影或參與相關的活動，我幾乎走遍了世界大部份的角落，看到很多本來物產豐富，山明水秀的地方變得殘破落後，民生貧困。而引致這些局面的原因，毫不例外都是戰爭。部落與部落的戰爭，國家與國家之間的戰爭，不同宗教信仰之間的戰爭。

無論是怎樣的戰爭，都有一個共同的目的，就是人類殺死人類。就算好不容易結束戰爭過去，但戰爭做成的破壞和貧窮仍會繼續折磨戰火餘生的人民幾十年。然後當大部分人努力地在戰後的廢墟中重建家園的時候，舊的爭論又會引發新的戰爭。

United Nations   Nations Unies
NEW YORK   GENÈVE

對於即將來臨的 2000 年，我有一個卑微卻又奢侈的願望，就是希望人類不再有戰爭。我說這個願望卑微而又奢侈，是因為每個人都毫無疑問地明白戰爭為人類帶來災難，但地球上仍舊每一天都有戰爭在發生。

我希望也不必等到 2000 年的來臨，就從今天起，無論是部落與部落之間為了食物和資源的分配，為是國家與國家之間對土地的爭奪，對意識形態的爭論，甚至宗教與宗教之間為了信仰不同的神的爭執，都要盡最大的努力避免訴之於戰爭，而用心不氣和，冷靜理性的態度來解決。

UNITED NATIONS

問題是我這樣說的時候，連我自己都覺得天真得可笑，可想而知希望以傳統的智慧來消除戰爭並不容易。但人類自稱萬物之靈，數百年來，從哥崙布抱著一個地球是圓的觀念，摸索著找到新大陸，到今天的太空漫遊，我們的知識就是因為破除了無數成見而取得無法想像的進展。難道在即將來臨 2000 年裡，我們沒有勇氣破除這個 —— 任何爭執最後只能以武力解決 —— 成見？

如果可以破除這個成見，人類的 2000 年一定是一個史無前例地向前飛躍發展的年代。

如果人類有足夠的智慧的話。

Jackie Chan
Jackie Chan
HONG KONG 1-7-97

ART LINKLETTER

Birthplace:
Moose Jaw, Canada

Age at the Millennium: 88

One of the first persons to host live television, Art Linkletter was an institution in the 1950s. His work includes *House Party* and *People are Funny*. His biggest show, *Kids Say the Darndest Things*, became a best-selling book.

12

United Nations   **Nations Unies**
NEW YORK   GENÈVE

6/18/97

I have noted, with considerable alarm, the decay
and turmoil in the Western countries of the world
among families. The pace of our lives and the many
distractions as well as the growing dis-equilibrium
of the strength of the traditional family is a certain
marker for the weakening of the entire social fabric.
Divorce, single family parenting with no father in
the household and the movement of people away from
familiar surroundings all contribute to this breakdown. I predict that the eventual restoration of the
nuclear family and the triumph of parental obligations
and filial devotion will correct this abberation in
the human condition and that we will come back together
in the universal need for family unity and strength.

Art Linkletter

©
UNITED
NATIONS

An improvisational comedian in Europe in the 1970s, John Ratzenberger returned to the United States in 1982 to audition for the role Cliff Claven on a new sitcom called *Cheers*. Ratzenberger would become a household face during the show's eleven-year run.

Birthplace:
Bridgeport, Conn.

Age at the Millennium: 53

JOHN RATZENBERGER

United Nations   Nations Unies
NEW YORK   GENÈVE

To Millennium Committee —
These are some thoughts —
Unless America focuses her might to education, the U.S. will lose its place among nations / The Internet and its offspring will do to Television what T.V. did to Radio. There will Be a U.N. initiative to stem the tide of disease from central Africa. A cure will be found for diabetes. Storms the size of Hurricane Andrew will be commonplace. Wars will be fought over clean water sources.

A plan will be considered to put a roof over Times Sq. China will be next super power

Address

John Ratzenberger
Vashon Is. WA
6-97

To Millennium Committee—
These are some thoughts—
Unless America focuses her might to education, the U.S. will lose its place among nations. The Internet and its offspring will do to Television what T.V. did to Radio. There will be a U.N. initiative to stem the tide of disease from central Africa. A cure will be found for diabetes. Storms the size of Hurricane Andrew will be commonplace. Wars will be fought over clean water sources. A plan will be considered to put a roof over Times Square. China will be next super power.

NORMAN LEAR

Birthplace:
New Haven, Conn.

Age at the Millennium: 78

A groundbreaking television producer, Norman Lear revolutionized the sitcom by injecting controversial social issues into his scripts. His vastly successful *All in the Family* was followed by *The Jeffersons, Sanford & Son, Maude,* and *Mary Hartman,* among others.

United Nations   Nations Unies
NEW YORK   GENÈVE

IT WILL BE TRUE IN THE NEXT MILLENNIUM AS IT WAS IN THIS, THAT ETERNAL VIGILENCE IS THE PRICE OF LIBERTY. PAY THE PRICE.

LOS ANGELES, CALIFORNIA
JANUARY 20, 1998

Address

©
UNITED
NATIONS

Photo by Ron Sachs/CNP/Archive Photos

Both an acclaimed actress and singer, Leslie Uggams began her singing career at a young age with Mitch Miller. Her acting debut in *Roots* was highly praised, and Uggams soon turned to Broadway where she has won several Tony Awards.

Birthplace:
New York, N.Y.

Age at the Millennium: 57

LESLIE UGGAMS

United Nations   **Nations Unies**
NEW YORK   GENÈVE

By the year 3,000, it is my opinion that for the first time in modern history a new race of people within the borders of The United States of America will be recognized by anthropologists from around the world.

This new race will be the culmination of One thousand two hundred and twenty-two years, of Asian, African, European and South American immigration to The United States of America.

At that time we will be free of the chains of past prejudice and proud of the historical struggle for equality.

Address

Leslie Uggams
July 1997

© UNITED NATIONS

By the year 3,000, it is my opinion that for the first time in modern history a new race of people within the borders of The United States of America will be recognized by anthropologists from around the world. This new race will be the culmination of One thousand two hundred and twenty-two years, of Asian, African, European and South American immigration to The United States of America.

At that time we will be free of the chains of past prejudice and proud of the historical struggle for equality.

KEVIN SORBO

Birthplace:
Mound, Minn.

Age at the
Millennium: 42

The star of the world's highest rated syndicated television series, *Hercules: The Legendary Journeys*, Kevin Sorbo has developed a dedicated following since his debut in 1994. As Hercules, Sorbo performs most of his own stunts and action scenes.

United Nations   Nations Unies
NEW YORK   GENÈVE

WHILE THE 20TH CENTURY WAS PREOCCUPIED WITH LENGTHENING THE HUMAN LIFETIME, OFTEN WITH LITTLE REGARD TO QUALITY OF LIFE, THE NEW MILLENNIUM WILL GIVE BIRTH TO A GREATER UNDERSTANDING AND GROWING INTEREST IN FITNESS, EXERCISE, AND NUTRITION. NOT ONLY LONGEVITY, BUT ALSO LIFESTYLE WILL BE ADDRESSED EARLIER, AND MORE SERIOUSLY IN SCHOOLS, IN THE HOPES OF GIVING OUR CHILDREN A CHANCE FOR MORE FULFILLING AND HAPPIER LIVES.

Address

KEVIN SORBO
MOUND, MINNESOTA,
APRIL 25, 1998

© UNITED NATIONS

While the 20th century was preoccupied with lengthening the human lifetime, often with little regard to quality of life, the new millennium will give birth to a greater understanding and growing interest in fitness, exercise, and nutrition. Not only longevity, but also lifestyle will be addressed earlier, and more seriously in schools, in the hopes of giving our children a chance for more fulfilling and happier lives.

A popular television actor, Daniel J. Travanti is best known for the role of Captain Furillo in the 1980s series *Hill Street Blues*. Also a veteran stage actor, Travanti has frequently appeared in various productions.

Birthplace:
Kenosha, Wis.

Age at the Millennium: 60

DANIEL J. TRAVANTI

United Nations   Nations Unies
NEW YORK   GENÈVE

I'M AFRAID THAT MACHINES WILL RULE OUR LIVES. AND RELIGION. BOTH ARE CONTROLS THAT DO NOT PROMOTE ART OR FREEDOM OF EXPRESSION OR CREATIVITY.

I AM GOING TO HOPE THAT LOVE AND RESPECT FOR ALL PEOPLE AND THE PLANET MOTIVATE OUR ACTIONS. I AM GOING TO HOPE THAT HUMANS WILL ADMIT THAT WE ARE THE ONLY CREATURES WHO DON'T FIT NATURE'S PERFECT SCHEMES, AND SEE THAT OUR PLACE ON EARTH IS TO PROTECT EVERYTHING: DIRT, MICROBES, BIRDS INSECTS, ANIMALS, TREES, WATER, AIR AND PEOPLE.

BUT I AM AFRAID WE WILL ONLY INTERFERE MORE. I HOPE I'M WRONG.

Address

DANIEL J. TRAVANTI
LAKE FOREST, ILLINOIS

© UNITED NATIONS

Daniel J Travanti

EARLE HYMAN

Birthplace:
Rocky Mount, N.C.

Age at the
Millennium: 74

A brilliant Shakespearean actor, Earle Hyman has been widely praised for his on-stage performances since the 1950s. He has appeared in several major Broadway productions, but is best known in Europe where he has won numerous awards.

United Nations   Nations Unies
NEW YORK   GENÈVE

In the next millenium I see a couple, a young man and a young woman standing forth as Citizens of the World because in their veins flows the blood of all the races. They stand forth in beauty and quiet assurance because they know that in their hearts, minds and hands rest limitless possibilities for progress in the Arts, Science, Philosophy and the true Brotherhood and Sisterhood of Man.

July 10, 1997 - SKÅNEVIK, NORWAY   Earle Hyman

Address

UNITED
NATIONS

In the next millennium I see a couple, a young man and a young woman standing forth as Citizens of the World because in their veins flows the blood of all the races. They stand forth in beauty and quiet assurance because they know that in their hearts, minds and hands rest limitless possibilities for progress in the Arts, Science, Philosophy and the true Brotherhood and Sisterhood of Man.

19   At the age of 27, Joanne Woodward received the Academy Award for Best Actress and later married fellow actor Paul Newman. Woodward's roles have earned her widespread praise and she is one of the few Americans to win at Cannes.

Birthplace:
Thomasville, Ga.

Age at the Millennium: 70

JOANNE WOODWARD

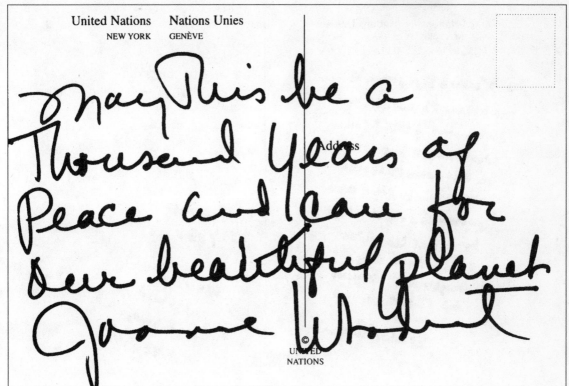

May this be a thousand years of peace and care for our beautiful planet.

SIR JOHN GIELGUD

Birthplace:
London, England

Age at the
Millennium: 96

One of the most commanding actors of the century, John Gielgud has performed on stage and film since 1921. Gielgud's classical British roles were later followed with numerous American movies and awards. In 1994 London's Globe Theatre was renamed after him.

20

United Nations   Nations Unies
NEW YORK   GENÈVE

As troubles seem to continue to assail us from every part of this world, may I pray that in the new millennium we may hope that a more

Address

February
1998.

Wotton
Underwood
Aylesbury
Bucks.

John Gielgud.

©
UNITED
NATIONS

As troubles seem to continue to assail us from every part of this world, may I pray that in the new millennium we may hope that a more peaceful solution may be found to make the future less fraught with dangers and tribulations.

Perhaps the most successful entertainer in the history of television, Bill Cosby's career has spanned thirty years as not just a beloved comic actor but also as a producer. Cosby has received eight Emmy Awards.

Birthplace:
Germantown, Pa.

Age at the
Millennium: 63

BILL COSBY

United Nations   Nations Unies
NEW YORK   GENÈVE

We will or are responsible for the next and the next. Let us respect good things and live on. — Bill Cosby

Address

UNITED NATIONS

We will be or are responsible for the next and the next.
Let us respect good things and live on.

Photo by Archive Photos

ROGER EBERT

Birthplace:
Urbana, Ill.

Age at the
Millennium: 58

America's most famous film critic, Roger Ebert paired with fellow Chicagoan newspaperman Gene Siskel in 1976 to broadcast the first weekly movie reviews. Ebert has written nine books, and won Emmy and Pulitzer prizes.

United Nations   Nations Unies
NEW YORK   GENÈVE

Tribalism will die out and humans will cease to be victims of the us—vs. them mentality.

Roger Ebert.

©
UNITED
NATIONS

Address

Tribalism will die out and humans will cease to be victims of the us vs. them mentality.

Photo by Buena Vista Television.

23 In 1978, architect and journalist Bob Vila created a surprisingly successful home improvement show, *This Old House*, for PBS. Vila developed a cult following and subsequently began his current series, *Bob Vila's Home Again*.

Birthplace:
Miami, Fla.

Age at the Millennium: 54

BOB VILA

United Nations   Nations Unies
NEW YORK   GENÈVE

*I predict the demise
of the last 2 Communist
dictatorships — Cuba & N. Korea —
and the continued devel-
opment of free democratic
states throughout the world.*

Bob Vila

-Address

©
UNITED
NATIONS

I predict the demise of the last 2 Communist dictatorships—
Cuba & N. Korea—and the continued development of free democratic
states throughout the world.

RICHARD PRYOR

Birthplace:
Peoria, Ill.

Age at the
Millennium: 60

A giant of stand-up comedy, Richard Pryor pioneered the popularity of monologues meant to shock audiences with "street talk" and racial humor. The highest paid comedian of the early 1980s, Pryor was later sidetracked by a near-fatal burn injury.

United Nations   Nations Unies
NEW YORK   GENÈVE

Address

Love each other and avoid Prejudism (Racism) Richard Pryor.

Love each other and avoid Prejudism (Racism).

Phyllis Diller's renowned rapid punch lines and trademark hairstyle have made her an entertainment legend. In her fifty-year career, Diller has also appeared in twelve movies and has written five humor books.

Birthplace:
Lima, Ohio

Age at the Millennium: 83

PHYLLIS DILLER

United Nations   Nations Unies
NEW YORK   GENÈVE

July 17, 1997

The constants all through the centuries will be the same; wine, women and song. Other than that, life will be very different technologically. In the year 3000 the universe will be expanding as it will forever, infinitely. We will probe outer space but never find life as evolutionized as ours. We were not created by a deity. We created the deity in <u>our</u> image. Life began on this planet when the first ameba split. Mankind will still be seeking God, not accepting that God is a spirit; can't see it, touch it, only feel it. It's called LOVE.

Phyllis Diller

Birthplace:
New York, N.Y.

**Age at the
Millennium: 43**

David Caruso starred in the dramatic television series *NYPD Blue* for several years, gaining considerable fame. He left the show to pursue motion pictures and currently leads the series *Michael Hayes.*

United Nations   Nations Unies
NEW YORK   GENÈVE

"OUR BLATANT
DISREGARD FOR
EACH OTHER WILL BECOME
A SPORT"

D.c.

Address

©
UNITED
NATIONS

Our blatant disregard for each other will become a sport.

One of the first performers on *Saturday Night Live,* Joe Piscopo left the groundbreaking series after four years. A popular comedian, Piscopo's films include *Living Dangerously, Wise Guys,* and several HBO specials.

Birthplace:
Passaic, N.J.

Age at the
Millennium: 49

JOE PISCOPO

United Nations   Nations Unies
NEW YORK   GENÈVE

my predictions for the 3rd Millennium:

Peace in the middle East, all disease will be eradicated and the world's #1 vacation destination will be a tour of the rest stops along the New Jersey Turnpike...

Joe Piscopo

NEWARK, NJ
1998.

Address

Greetings from
NEW JERSEY, USA!
1·9·98

©
UNITED
NATIONS

My prediction for the 3rd Millennium: Peace in the Middle East, all disease will be eradicated and the world's #1 vacation destination will be a tour of the rest stops along the New Jersey Turnpike . . .

NORM ABRAM

Birthplace: Woonsocket, R.I.

Age at the Millennium: 51

Described as a "carpenter turned celebrity," Norm Abram began his television career in 1979 and still appears on *This Old House*. A master carpenter, Abram also hosts his own show, *The New Yankee Workshop*, and has written six books.

United Nations   Nations Unies
NEW YORK   GENÈVE

My hope for the future is that more individuals will be inspired to become fine craftsmen so that we can continue to restore, preserve and maintain our architectural treasures of the past as well as build new ones for future generations to appreciate. Technology over the last several decades has brought us more sophisticated tools, but no matter how sophisticated the tools, good craftsmanship comes from the mind, eyes and hands of the dedicated craftsman.

Norm Abram
Boston, Massachusetts
March 9, 1998

©
UNITED
NATIONS

Photo by Keller & Keller

An expert architectural renovator, Steve Thomas gained national fame in 1989 as the new host of the hit PBS show *This Old House*. Thomas is also an accomplished sailor and an author on historic renovations.

Birthplace:
Pramona, Calif.

Age at the
Millennium: 47

STEVE THOMAS

The world can be an unspeakably violent place, where greed and ambition rip the fragile tissue of civility like a jagged knife through human skin. Given that human beings have remained the same throughout the last millennium this is not likely to change in the next. Those who suffer most are the children. So, given my business is houses, rather than a prediction for the next hundred years, I have a hope, and a grand one: that every child in the world can experience the security of a home. Be it a mud hut or a mansion, a home is a physical place which offers food, a bed to sleep in without fear of violence, a space to nurture the mind, to dream and let the spirit expand, a place filled with love of a family. Every child who grows up in a home like this is likely to be considerate of himself, the earth and his fellow creatures, thus, although it is a naive hope it is one we must try to realize.

Boston, Massachusetts
July 1997

STEVE THOMAS
Host of *"This Old House"*

Photo by Richard Howard for WGBH Boston

JANE SEYMOUR

Birthplace:
Hillington, England

Age at the
Millennium: 49

Jane Seymour is perhaps best known as the star of the popular television series *Dr. Quinn, Medicine Woman*. The Emmy Award–winning Seymour has also had a successful film career, including a James Bond film and the miniseries *East of Eden*.

United Nations   Nations Unies
NEW YORK   GENÈVE

THE THIRD MILLENNIUM:

CALL ME A COCK-EYED OPTIMIST, SOMEHOW I HAVE FAITH THAT IN 1000 YEARS MANKIND WILL FIND THE STRENGTH AND WISDOM THAT WILL HELP ACHIEVE WORLD PEACE AND HARMONY. WITH THE MODERN WORLD'S SPIRALING POPULATION EXPECTATIONS ANY ALTERNATIVE IS SIMPLY TOO AWFUL TO CONTEMPLATE. WE WILL SIMPLY HAVE TO FIND A WAY TO CONTROL THE POPULATION AND DEFEAT OUR BASER INSTINCTS.

Address

Jane Seymour

JANE SEYMOUR
BEVERLY HILLS, CALIFORNIA 1998

©
UNITED
NATIONS

Photo by Popperfoto / Archive Photos

An actor on Broadway at a young age, Bruce Dern also played various supporting roles on television before receiving motion picture parts. In 1978 he was nominated for an Academy Award, and has built a loyal public following from his film roles.

Birthplace:
Chicago, Ill.

Age at the Millennium: 64

BRUCE DERN

United Nations   Nations Unies
NEW YORK   GENÈVE

I WOULD HOPE THAT ALL ETHNIC AND COLOR LINES of DIVERSITY THROUGHT THE WORLD; BE totally eliminated as to ANY SOCIAL, ECONOMIC OR VALUE JUDGEMENT LINES. BOTH IN REALISTIC EYES AND THE EYES OF GOD.

Hopefully THE WORLD will Achieve its RACIAL AND ATHNIC POTENTIAL in A PEACEFULL Humanitarian WAY.

THAT'S what to see for the 21st century —

Thanks for The chance to Express myself AND give AN opinion.

Bruce Dern

Address

6/11/97
MALIBU, CALIFORNIA
U.S.A.

© UNITED NATIONS

I would hope that all ethnic and color lines of diversity throughout the world; be totally eliminated as to any social, economic or value judgement lines. Both in realistic eyes and the eyes of God.
Hopefully the world will achieve its racial and ethnic potential in a peaceful humanitarian way.

That's what I see for the 21st century—
Thanks for the chance to express myself and give an opinion.

Photo by Archive Photos

BUFFALO BOB SMITH

Birthplace:
Buffalo, N.Y.

Deceased 1998

One of the first persons ever to appear on television daily, Buffalo Bob Smith created the *Howdy Doody Show* in 1947. By 1960 he and his famed puppet were a household institution. Mr. Smith passed away in 1998 at the age of 80.

United Nations   Nations Unies
NEW YORK   GENÈVE

We sincerely hope that people in the next millennium will continue to remember that MF (MIT Feeling).

Address

It's How-dy Doo-dy time—ALWAYS!

©
UNITED
NATIONS

A stage and television actress, Joan Van Ark is best known for her four years on *Dallas* and thirteen years on *Knots Landing*. Van Ark has appeared in numerous television movies, and she continues to perform on Broadway and in London.

Birthplace:
New York, N.Y.

Age at the Millennium: 57

JOAN VAN ARK

United Nations   Nations Unies
NEW YORK   GENÈVE

It would be trite to wish what is on everyone's lips once a year: "Peace on Earth, goodwill toward men." But if I were to share what's really in my heart, my hope for the future is that what we now view as so horrific with Dr. Kevorkian and his "assisted suicides" will become an accepted option for terminally ill patients who have lost the quality of their life . . . And that medical assistance to gently guide a terminal patient to the 'next level,' will become an accepted choice in the next millennium.

Address

Joan Van Ark

©
UNITED
NATIONS

TIM ALLEN

Birthplace:
Denver, Colo.

Age at the
Millennium: 47

As the lead in one of television's most successfully running comedies, Tim Allen has branched out from his original sitcom *Home Improvement,* begun in 1991. Allen has starred in a number of films, including *Santa Clause* and *Jungle Man.*

United Nations   Nations Unies
NEW YORK   GENÈVE

'Eat all your vegetables' and take care of your neighbor.

Address

©
UNITED
NATIONS

'Eat all your vegetables' and take care of your neighbor.   *Photo by Archive Photos*

As the resident groundskeeper on O. J. Simpson's property, Kato Kaelin became a central witness in the century's most notorious murder investigation. Made famous by the trial, Kaelin later pursued various television and radio opportunities.

Birthplace:
Glendale, Calif.

Age at the Millennium: 40

KATO KAELIN

United Nations Nations Unies
NEW YORK GENÈVE

The Time you live on earth is short. Live with Real Love in your heart for your neighbor. ERASE HATE!!

I believe that between the years 2001 and 3000 a few things will happen.

1.) The Beatles find more lost recording session tapes under Ringo's sofa cushions.

2) KATO Kaelin will still be living His Fifteen minutes of FAME. YEAH!!

3) Love will Rule.

= KATO

Address

These thoughts were written on Sunday Agust 10, 1997 in Beverly Hills CA, USA on a very messy kitchen Table in an even messier apartment.

LOVY, Kato Kaeli

© UNITED NATIONS

P.S. Please check for spelling

The time you live on earth is short. Live with *Real Love in your heart for your neighbor.
ERASE HATE!!*
I believe that between the years 2001 and 3000 a few things will happen.

1.) The Beatles find more lost recording session tapes under Ringo's sofa cushions.

2.) Kato Kaelin will still be living his fifteen minutes of fame. Yeah!!

3.) Love will Rule.

These thoughts were written on Sunday August 10, 1997 in Beverly Hills CA, USA on a very messy kitchen table in an even messier apartment.

JOAN COLLINS

Birthplace:
London, England

**Age at the
Millennium: 67**

A legendary actress on both sides of the Atlantic, Joan Collins has appeared in dozens of films since the 1950s. Her eight-year lead role in television's *Dynasty* made her one of America's favorite villains.

36

United Nations   Nations Unies
NEW YORK   GENÈVE

My prediction for the next millennium is that mankind will become almost totally reliant on the technology of computers.

I believe that this reliance will destroy mankind's greatest assets, the ability to fend for oneself and think for oneself.

In the past 100 years, many of the things we have taken for granted have been lost. The ability to grow food, build accomodation and the ability to repair anything. Our society now is predisposed to built-in obsolescence and mankind's weaknesses. I only hope that this does not happen to man.

Address

JOAN COLLINS, O.B.E.
London, England
1998

© UNITED NATIONS

37 The most accomplished comedian in history, Bob Hope has performed in seven decades of film and television. He also entertained American troops from WWII to Desert Storm. Befriended by nine presidents, he is the only civilian ever declared a veteran by Congress.

**Birthplace:
London, England**

**Age at the
Millennium: 97**

BOB HOPE

United Nations   Nations Unies
NEW YORK   GENÈVE

```
I'm not big on predicting.
If I was, I'd be at the
track every day.

But, if the new millennium
is going to be worth anything
there has to be laughter...
and a lot of it.
```

Address

©
UNITED
NATIONS

SAMUEL FULLER

Birthplace:
Worcester, Mass.

Deceased 1997

A controversial filmmaker, Samuel Fuller's movies broke new ground for artfulness and satire. Less known in America, Fuller did much of his work in France to wide acclaim. Mr. Fuller passed away in 1997 at age 86.

United Nations   Nations Unies
NEW YORK   GENÈVE

*"Science sans conscience n'est que ruine de l'ame." (Rabelais)
While the exponential explosion of technology and science insures that the next millennium will hold forth a future for mankind that is today impossible to comprehend, I am confident that the historical contexts of war and peace will be transcended by a totally revolutionized global, if not interplanetary order.*

Samuel Fuller
aug. 1997

"Science sans conscience n'est que ruine de l'ame." (Rabelais)

While the exponential explosion of technology and science insures that the next millennium will hold forth a future for mankind that is today impossible to comprehend, I am confident that the historical contexts of war and peace will be transcended by a totally revolutionized global, if not interplanetary order.

Photo by Curtis Hanson

39 An acclaimed actress and former *Vogue* model, Anjelica Huston received an Academy Award for her first major film role in *Prizzi's Honor,* directed by her father John Huston. She received another Oscar nomination in 1990 for her role in *The Grifters.*

Birthplace:
Los Angeles, Calif.

Age at the
Millennium: 49

ANJELICA HUSTON

United Nations   Nations Unies
NEW YORK   GENÈVE

The cure for Cancer
More theme Parks
More Pollution
The cure for Aids
Peace in Ireland

Anjelica Huston

Address

VENICE - CA

January 13th 1998

©
UNITED
NATIONS

The cure for Cancer
More theme Parks
More Pollution
The cure for AIDS
Peace in Ireland

Photo by Popperfoto / Archive Photos

ARTHUR HILLER

Birthplace:
Edmonton, Canada

**Age at the
Millennium: 77**

One of television's earliest film directors, Arthur Hiller began his career with the *Alfred Hitchcock Presents* series. He has directed numerous movies from the 1960s to the 1990s and received an Oscar nomination for his 1970 film *Love Story*.

40

United Nations   Nations Unies
NEW YORK   GENEVE

Per attached letter:

In the 2000's one person will be able to sit in front of a computer and create an entire movie. He or she will digitally create characters with the looks, styles, movement and emotions that he or she desire the character to have. Then they will be digitally staged on sets and against backgrounds all created on the computer. Yes, a wonderful new way of telling a story but I hope we won't lose the heart and soul of filmmaking that comes from so many wonderfully creative juices coming together, mixing, and out of it comes this new entity – a movie.

In the 2000's we will see the loss of the U.S. and Canada being the best countries to live in. That will come about from fractionalization of the U.S. and possibly Canada by the terrible need of many ethnic groups not just to respect their heritage and still be part of this wonderful "melting pot" we live in, but to be the #1 group and in control. Gone will be the days of caring for each other as human beings, and respecting each other's cultural contributions as well as individual contributions. Oh yes, we will all want democracy -- as long as our group is in charge and it's our way.

©
UNITED
NATIONS   *Arthur Hiller*

41   A Hollywood giant, Michael Douglas has played the leading man in such blockbusters as *Romancing the Stone, Fatal Attraction, Basic Instinct, Disclosure,* and *The American President.* In 1988 Douglas won an Oscar for *Wall Street.*

Birthplace: New Brunswick, N.J.

Age at the Millennium: 56

MICHAEL DOUGLAS

United Nations   Nations Unies
NEW YORK   GENÈVE

I hope the Millennium will finally bring us a nuclear free world!

Michael Douglas

© UNITED NATIONS

Address

I hope the Millennium will finally bring us a nuclear free world!   *Photo by Max Miller / Fotos International / Archive Photos*

HAL PRINCE

Birthplace:
New York, N.Y.

**Age at the
Millennium: 72**

One of the most successful producers in the
history of Broadway, Hal Prince's productions—
usually with the musical talent of Stephen
Sondheim—include *West Side Story*, *Fiddler on the
Roof,* and *Sweeney Todd.*

United Nations   Nations Unies
NEW YORK   GENÈVE

July 31 '97

*Our current obsession with technology
is a dead end — unless the next
Millennium renews our faith in the
unknown — the miraculous mystery
of Man's Soul.
I am at heart an optimist:
It will!*

Harold Prince
New York City U.S.A.

©
UNITED
NATIONS

Our current obsession with technology is a dead end—*unless the next
Millennium renews our faith in the unknown—the miraculous mystery
of Man's Soul.
I am at heart an optimist: It will!*

An institution to the world's "Trekkers," LeVar Burton has acted in many roles but is best known for the science-conscious character Jordie in the second *Star Trek* television series. Besides new film roles, Burton is an author.

**Birthplace:
Landstuhl, Germany**

**Age at the
Millennium: 43**

LEVAR
BURTON

United Nations   **Nations Unies**
NEW YORK   GENÈVE

I predict that in the Next millennium the human species will make a great leap in our spiritual evolution and come into a more complete alignment with our true purpose here.

©
UNITED
NATIONS

Address

LeVar Burton
Los Angeles CA

9/97

I predict that in the next millennium the human species will make a great leap in our spiritual evolution and come into a more complete alignment with our true purpose here.

Photo by Archive Photos

BURGESS MEREDITH

Birthplace:
Cleveland, Ohio

Deceased 1997

Burgess Meredith first appeared in films in 1936. Having a trademark voice, he made numerous films and later appeared in over one hundred television shows. Mr. Meredith passed away in 1997 at age 89.

United Nations   Nations Unies
NEW YORK   GENÈVE

I don't know what tomorrow
(much less the Millenium!)
will bring. Life changes
frequently and drastically.

You enjoy it or endure it
one day at a time. But here
we have survived fires, floods,
mudslides and earthquakes.
The future will bring new
perils -- but we will win new
victories. So as I glance
toward the future we cannot
see, I say, "So far, so good!"

Address

Burgess Meredith
Malibu, California
1997

©
UNITED
NATIONS

Burgess Meredith

Chapter 2

Nobel Laureates

ARCHBISHOP DESMOND TUTU

Birthplace: Klerksdorp, South Africa

Age at the Millennium: 69

Archbishop Desmond Tutu pioneered the nonviolent protest against South Africa's apartheid system of racial segregation. Organizing worldwide sanctions, Tutu received the 1984 Nobel Peace Prize and later lobbied for the release of Nelson Mandela.

United Nations   Nations Unies
NEW YORK   GENÈVE

By Desmond Tutu
in Cape Town South Africa
Feb 1997.

There will be widespread peace.
International debts will be cancelled & poverty will be diminished.
The Arms race will be abolished as nations beat their swords into ploughshares.
We will commute between planet earth & other planets.

Address

Men & women will be truly equal
Human life will be revered & the environment spared.
There will be an explosion of technological excellence & innovation.
The arts, music, literature painting, drama will reach unprecedented heights.

© UNITED NATIONS

There will be widespread peace. International debts will be cancelled and poverty will be diminished. The arms race will be abolished as nations beat their swords into ploughshares. We will commute between planet earth and other planets. Men and women will be truly equal. Human life will be revered and the environment spared. There will be an explosion of technological excellence and innovation. The arts, music, literature, painting, drama will reach unprecedented heights.

Photo by Archive Photos

A three-term prime minister of Israel, Peres was first elected to the office in 1984. Later as foreign minister, he was a corecipient of the 1994 Nobel Peace Prize. Peres again became prime minister following Yitzhak Rabin's assassination.

Birthplace:
Wolozyn, Poland

Age at the Millennium: 77

SHIMON PERES

United Nations   Nations Unies
NEW YORK   GENÈVE

I believe that in the twenty-first century:

- Many life-sustaining enigmas will be unraveled: biotechnology will be at the forefront of scientific research.

- The lifespan of human beings will increase twofold.

- People will lead healthier lives and will be less prone to present-day diseases: many defects in the future will be corrected while it is still in its mother's womb: drugs will be developed to treat the principle diseases and old-age symptoms afflicting today's society, such as cancer, AIDS and senility.

- People will be able to select their own size, as well as the color of their skin and eyes.

- Time will be used differently: one third will be allocated to work: one third to leisure-related activities, such as sports, art and trips.

- Sightseeing tours will include the moon and stars.

- Spacecraft will be the most common vehicle for air travel.

- Luggage will be practically obsolete: throw-away clothes will be available.

©
UNITED NATIONS

United Nations   Nations Unies
NEW YORK   GENÈVE

- Addresses will be substituted by an electronic gadget including a T.V., fax, telephone and Internet. Communication systems will incorporate pictures, words, numbers and memory units.

- The ratio between land and sea will change: a large part of the seas and oceans will dry up, turning into populated areas, and a considerable amount of the available water will be exploited for irrigation and drinking purposes.

- The redirection of water will turn what was once deserts into blooming populated regions.

- New advances in the field of energy fission will decrease pollution and reduce the cost of energy.

- Land traffic will be governed by mobile roads.

- A global conditioned environment will be the norm.

- Borders, distances and distinctions will practically disappear.

- Every person will hold a moral historical identity card, and a scientific passport to a changing world.

©
UNITED NATIONS

United Nations   Nations Unies
NEW YORK   GENÈVE

- Every person will be able to act as guest or host, teacher or pupil, as required.

- Wars will cease: human energy will be directed for creative purposes, in every sphere of science, art and relaxation.

- People will learn how to mobilize their inner potentials, to produce higher skills in all walks of life.

- Space will become of many industries, services and defenses. A cleaner globe will serve as the living room of human kind.

Address

Shimon Peres

16. 6. 97

©
UNITED NATIONS

DR. ARNO PENZIAS

Birthplace:
Munich, Germany

Age at the
Millennium: 67

A prominent scientist and executive at Lucent Technologies, Arno Penzias earned the Nobel Prize for Physics in 1978 by proving that cosmic microwave radiation exists in outer space. This greatly advanced the Big Bang Theory.

United Nations   Nations Unies
NEW YORK   GENÈVE

1) Our detailed understanding of the molecular basis of life will make us so adept at fighting diseases that we will need to address problems created by their absence.

2) We'll make all our "fossil fuels" out of carbon dioxide and water, using nuclear fusion as the primary energy source.

3) Computers with the power of today's best machines will cost no more than a postage stamp and be just as plentiful.

4) At that point we'll still have nine centuries more to go.

Arno Penzias
San Francisco
April 1997

UNITED
NATIONS

As the codiscover of DNA (with Francis Crick), James Dewey Watson made the century's most revolutionary advancement in genetics. Watson received the 1961 Nobel Prize for Physiology/Medicine and later directed the Cold Spring Harbor Laboratory.

Birthplace:
Chicago, Ill.

Age at the Millennium: 72

DR. JAMES DEWEY WATSON

United Nations   Nations Unies
NEW YORK   GENÈVE

1 January '98

During the next millennium the biological roles of virtually all the approximately 100,000 human genes will be established allowing the pinpointing of the genes which underlie the high level cognitive capacity of the human brain.

James D. Wd

Address

© UNITED NATIONS

During the next millennium the biological roles of virtually all the approximately 100,000 human genes will be established allowing the pinpointing of the genes which underlie the high level cognitive capacity of the human brain.

Photo by Margot Bennett

DR. JEROME KARLE

Birthplace:
New York, N.Y.

Age at the Millennium: 83

A biophysicist at the Naval Research Laboratory, Jerome Karle partnered with Herbert Hauptman to devise methods for identifying the three-dimensional crystal structures of various molecules. Karle received the 1985 Nobel Prize for Chemistry.

United Nations   Nations Unies
NEW YORK   GENÈVE

If humans continue to increase the earth's population, destroy the environment and produce children whose lives are devoid of love, self-respect, culture and respect for the dignity of all others, we can expect an increasing loss of quality of life, much suffering and violence, and a return to dark ages. If these current, self-destructive, large-scale assaults on our earth and its societies are sufficiently curtailed, science, technology and widespread rational thought and ethics should be able to bring the quality of life to unprecedented, high levels. I am not able to predict which way our world will proceed.

© UNITED NATIONS

Address

Jerome Karle
Washington, D.C.

May, 1997

A geneticist at the National Institutes of Health and University of Texas, Michael Brown partnered with Joseph Goldstein to identify the metabolism of cholesterol deficiencies in heart disease. Brown received the 1985 Nobel Prize for Physiology/Medicine.

Birthplace:
New York, N.Y.

Age at the Millennium: 59

DR. MICHAEL S. BROWN

United Nations   Nations Unies
NEW YORK   GENÈVE

In the third millenium the greatest challenge to humanity will emerge from the ability to control by chemical means the thought processes of human beings. Can society cope with the knowledge that human thought results from a chemical reaction and that it can be manipulated as easily

as one can manipulate the blood sugar?

Michael S Brown

Feb 9, 1998

Dallas, Texas

Address

© UNITED NATIONS

In the third millennium the greatest challenge to humanity will emerge from the ability to control by chemical means the thought processes of human beings. Can society cope with the knowledge that human thought results from a chemical reaction and that it can be manipulated as easily as one can manipulate the blood sugar?

DR. LEON N. COOPER

Birthplace:
New York, N.Y.

Age at the Millennium: 70

A physicist at Brown University, Leon Cooper proved a theory governing how certain electrons are paired, now known as "Cooper pairs." His contribution to the theory of superconductivity earned him the 1972 Nobel Prize for Physics.

United Nations   Nations Unies   Brown University Rhode Island
NEW YORK   GENÈVE   USA   May 1997

It's easier to predict what will happen in the next thousand years than what will happen next week—

so:

(I) Most of the diseases that plague us today will be cured — but others will emerge. Hopefully we'll be able to deal with them before they destroy us

(II) Thinking machines will be developed — machines that reason and perhaps are conscious. We will communicate with them as with other humans

(III) We will find a way to live forever

(IV) We will continue to complain that things are not as good as they used to be

(V) If we're lucky, we'll survive

I've run out of space so — to the human race Good Luck

Leon N Cooper

It's easier to predict what will happen in the next thousand years than what will happen next week—so:

(I) Most of the diseases that plague us today will be cured—but others will emerge. Hopefully we'll be able to deal with them before they destroy us.

(II) Thinking machines will be developed—machines that reason and perhaps are conscious. We will communicate with them as with other humans.

(III) We will find a way to live forever.

(IV) We will continue to complain that things are not as good as they used to be.

(V) If we're lucky, we'll survive.

I've run out of space so—to the human race Good Luck.

As one of the world's foremost experts on magnetic resonance, Richard Ernst has taught in both Europe and America. Ernst holds numerous patents for his inventions, and was awarded the 1991 Nobel Prize for Chemistry.

Birthplace:
Zurich, Switzerland

Age at the Millennium: 67

DR. RICHARD R. ERNST

United Nations   Nations Unies   **MY PREDICTION:** After the first millennium of the municipal communities, the second one of the nations, we will enter a third millennium of the global community. Conflicts will no longer be settled between nations but between social groupings, between the haves and the have-nots. The fights for survival might become increasingly cruel and costly. The free market system will have to be severely modified with penalties taking into account all conceivable adverse side effects. Numerous variations of a constrained global market system will be tried out, most of them leading deeper and deeper into economical and ecological disasters, until, finally, a self regulating system will be found that allows for an almost unlimited survival of mankind, although with drastically reduced population numbers, living standard, and individual freedom. Hopefully, our present excessive materialistic wealth will be replaced by a wealth of cultural creativity and productivity. However, a self-induced disaster that wipes out all previous cultural achievements is not inconceivable either.

RICHARD R. ERNST, CHEMISTRY © NOBEL PRIZE 1991
Zürich, 24 January 1998

UNITED NATIONS   Richard R. E

MY PREDICTION: *After the first millennium of the municipal communities, the second one of the nations, we will enter a third millennium of the global community. Conflicts will no longer be settled between nations but between social groupings, between the haves and the have-nots. The fights for survival might become increasingly cruel and costly. The free market system will have to be severely modified with penalties taking into account all conceivable adverse side effects. Numerous variations of a constrained global market system will be tried out, most of them leading deeper and deeper into economical and ecological disasters, until, finally, a self regulating system will be found that allows for an almost unlimited survival of mankind, although with drastically reduced population numbers, living standard, and individual freedom. Hopefully, our present excessive materialistic wealth will be replaced by a wealth of cultural creativity and productivity. However, a self-induced disaster that wipes out all previous cultural achievements is not inconceivable either.*

DR. HARRY MARKOWITZ

Birthplace:
Chicago, Ill.

Age at the Millennium: 73

A former executive at IBM, Harry Markowitz established groundbreaking theories regarding rational market behavior and investment activity. He also wrote several computer program languages. In 1990 Markowitz received the Nobel Prize for Economics.

United Nations   Nations Unies
NEW YORK   GENÈVE

Extrapolating the fast rate of technological advance, with its potential for great good or great evil, and the uncertain advance or decline in human morals, there is an uncomfortably high probability the next millennium will witness some form of mass destruction caused by man. Perhaps there are ways to reduce this probability

Harry Markowitz
San Diego, CA.
May 1997

© UNITED NATIONS

Extrapolating the fast rate of technological advance, with its potential for great good or great evil, and the uncertain advance or decline in human morals, there is an uncomfortably high probability the next millennium will witness some form of mass destruction caused by man. Perhaps there are ways to reduce this probability.

One of the greatest writers of the century, Nadine Gordimer has drawn from her South African homeland experiences to write numerous novels that eloquently deal with racism and freedom. Gordimer received the 1991 Nobel Prize for Literature.

Birthplace:
Transvaal, South Africa

Age at the Millennium: 77

NADINE GORDIMER

Johannesburg, South Africa 2/2/98

United Nations   Nations Unies
NEW YORK   GENÈVE

My hope is that with the 21st Century, in the spirit of what Jawaharlal Nehru called 'the ceaseless adventure of man', we dedicate ourselves to take control of the achievements of the 20th Century. That we question and reflect upon what has been done in the field of knowledge — scientific, technological, environmental, medical — what we have lived through, what has been gained at great cost of

Address

human suffering in the splitting of the atom, and must be then pursued to advance the quality of human life.

Nadine Gordimer

For the Millennium

©
UNITED
NATIONS

My hope is that with the 21st Century, in the spirit of what Jawaharlal Nehru called 'the ceaseless adventure of man', we dedicate ourselves to take control of the achievements of the 20th Century. That we question and reflect upon what has been done in the field of knowledge—scientific, technological, environmental, medical—what we have lived through, what has been gained at great cost of human suffering in the splitting of the atom, and must be then pursued to advance the quality of human life.

Photo by Horst Tappe / Archive Photos

LECH WALESA

**Birthplace:
Popowa, Poland**

**Age at the
Millennium: 57**

As the often-jailed leader of Poland's anti-communist Solidarity movement, Lech Walesa received the Nobel Peace Prize in 1983. His efforts were a major force in the collapse of the Iron Curtain. Walesa later became the first freely elected president of Poland.

United Nations   Nations Unies
NEW YORK   GENÈVE

*Settling the
issues of religious
dimension of man.*

1997

1.50 ZŁ · POLSKA   JAN PAWEŁ II   KRAKÓW

Address

Millenium Committee of New York
Attention: David J. Kristof
Box 20292
Dag Hammarskjold C.C.
New York, NY 10017   U.S.A.

©
UNITED
NATIONS

Settling the issues of the religious dimension of man.   *Photo by Imapress / Archive Photos*

An expert biologist of DNA and RNA analysis, Berg discovered a way to introduce foreign genes into bacteria, one of the earliest examples of genetic engineering. In 1980 Berg was awarded the Nobel Prize for Chemistry.

Birthplace:
New York, N.Y.

Age at the Millennium: 74

DR. PAUL BERG

United Nations
NEW YORK

Nations Unies
GENÈVE

Within the first century of the next millennium we shall have definitive proof of The existence of life outside our solar system. Such life forms will, whatever their appearance, rely on The same chemical and physical principles That govern life on earth.

Paul Berg
Stanford University, California
April 30, 1997

©
UNITED NATIONS

Within the first century of the next millennium we shall have definitive proof of the existence of life outside our solar system. Such life forms will, whatever their appearance, rely on the same chemical and physical principles that govern life on earth.

SIR DEREK H. R. BARTON

Birthplace:
Gravesend, England

Deceased 1998

Sir Derek Barton greatly advanced chemical analysis by adding a third dimension, conformational analysis. Barton received the 1969 Nobel Prize for Chemistry and was later knighted. Sir Derek Barton passed away in 1998 at age 79.

United Nations   Nations Unies
NEW YORK   GENÈVE

I predict that Molecular Biologists will find out how to stop the ageing process. Then we can all live forever. The world population will grow ad infinitum. A real problem!

Address

Derek H. R. Barton,
Dept. of Chemistry,
Texas A&M Univ
Tx
July 23rd, 1997.

UNITED NATIONS

I predict that Molecular Biologists will find out how to stop the aging process. Then we can all live forever. The world population will grow ad infinitum. *A real problem!*

Photo by James Lyle, Texas A&M University

A biophysicist at the Naval Research Laboratory, Herbert Hauptman partnered with Jerome Karle to devise methods for identifying the three-dimensional crystal structures of various molecules. Hauptman received the 1985 Nobel Prize for Chemistry.

Birthplace:
New York, N.Y.

Age at the Millennium: 83

DR. HERBERT A. HAUPTMAN

United Nations   Nations Unies
NEW YORK   GENÈVE

HOPE FOR THE FUTURE – THAT THE PEOPLES OF THE WORLD WILL AT LONG LAST COME TO RECOGNIZE THAT THE UNIVERSE IS A REALIZATION OF A LOGICAL STRUCTURE PERMITTING A RATIONAL DESCRIPTION, THAT THERE IS NO PLACE FOR BELIEF IN THE SUPER-NATURAL, AND THAT NO EVIDENCE EXISTS FOR BELIEF IN AN ALL KNOWING, ALL POWERFUL INTELLIGENCE.

Address

Herbert A. Hauptman
14 January 1998.
Buffalo, New York

©
UNITED
NATIONS

DR. GLENN T. SEABORG

Birthplace:
Ishpeming, Mich.

Age at the Millennium: 88

A Manhattan Project scientist alongside Einstein and Oppenheimer, Glenn Seaborg produced plutonium. He discovered and named five other radioactive elements. Seaborg received the 1951 Nobel Prize for Chemistry and later headed the Atomic Energy Commission.

United Nations   Nations Unies
NEW YORK   GENÈVE

Address

> *Drugs that will improve intelligence*
> *Glenn T. Seaborg*
> *April, 1997*
> *Berkeley, California*

©
UNITED
NATIONS

Drugs that will improve intelligence.   *Photo by Lawrence Berkeley National Lab.*

61 One of the greatest genetic scientists of the century, Arthur Kornberg was the first to synthesize nonreplicating DNA and to create a biologically active viral DNA. Kornberg received the Nobel Prize for Physiology/Medicine in 1959.

Birthplace:
New York, N.Y.

———

Age at the Millennium: 82

DR. ARTHUR KORNBERG

———

United Nations   Nations Unies
NEW YORK   GENÈVE

12 January '98

Inasmuch as the future is not predicted, but rather invented, I hope that the creativity of individuals for invention — scientific, artistic, industrial — will be nurtured by future societies worldwide. No one can predict the outcome of human intelligence properly applied.

Arthur Kornberg

Address Arthur Kornberg
Department of Biochemistry
Stanford University,
Stanford, CA

©
UNITED
NATIONS

Inasmuch as the future is not predicted, but rather invented, I hope that the creativity of individuals for invention—scientific, artistic, industrial—will be nurtured by future societies worldwide. No one can predict the outcome of human intelligence properly applied.

DR. FREDERICK SANGER

Birthplace:
Rendcombe, England

Age at the
Millennium: 82

Cambridge's greatest chemist, Frederick Sanger became the first person to receive a Nobel Prize twice (Chemistry, 1958 and 1980). Sanger greatly advanced insulin's effectiveness by identifying its amino acids and later found ways to identify nucleic acid structures.

United Nations   Nations Unies
NEW YORK   GENÈVE

In my own subject (DNA sequencing) the complete sequence of the human genome will be finished soon but understanding it will take longer. By 3000 we shall probably understand it and how the human body works in considerable detail, making considerable improvements in medical practice, which will be devoted more to improving living than to prolonging life. However the average lifespan will be around 100 years.

I think some time in the next millennium politicians will come to their senses and by 3000 there will be a strong world government & international police force, capable of settling disputes. National forces will be outlawed as will nuclear weapons. Population will be controlled and will be considerably reduced, hopefully by peaceful means.

J. Sanger.

June 1997

Address

Cambridge
England

© UNITED NATIONS

In my own subject (DNA sequencing) the complete sequence of the human genome will be finished soon but understanding it will take longer. By 3000 we shall probably understand it and how the human body works in considerable detail, making considerable improvements in medical practice, which will be devoted more to improving living than to prolonging life. However the average lifespan will be around 100 years.

I think some time in the next millennium politicians will come to their senses and by 3000 there will be a strong world government and international police force, capable of settling disputes. National forces will be outlawed as will nuclear weapons. Population will be controlled and will be considerably reduced, hopefully by peaceful means.

63

A prominent chemistry professor in both Europe and the United States, Ilya Prigogine received the 1977 Nobel Prize for Chemistry for his work in statistical mechanics and thermodynamics. Prigogine was later knighted in his native Belgium.

Birthplace:
Moscow, Russia

Age at the
Millennium: 83

VISCOUNT ILYA PRIGOGINE

United Nations   Nations Unies
NEW YORK   GENÈVE

We are in a period of transition. We are opening a new page of the history of mankind. Nobody can predict the future. However it may be hoped that the next millenium will see the emergence of a multipolar, multicultural world in which the men will have more opportunity to manifest their creativity. The past is full of violence. Our hope is in the future. Science and technology have to become instruments of cultural diffusion to make this hope a reality.

I. Prigogine

Brussels, May 21, 1997

DR. MANFRED EIGEN

Birthplace:
Bochum, Germany

**Age at the
Millennium: 73**

One of Europe's greatest chemists, Manfred Eigen developed processes for observing and analyzing rapid chemical reactions. Eigen became director of the prestigious Max Planck Institute in 1964 and received the Nobel Prize for Chemistry in 1967.

United Nations   Nations Unies
NEW YORK   GENÈVE

The evolution from man to mankind is still in its infancy. Its main goal will be global cooperation and a total ban of wars. I do hope, the coming millennium will bring us closer to this destination.

Göttingen, Germany. 1997

© UNITED NATIONS

Address

To the
Millennium Committee
of New York, LLC
Dag Hammarskjold
Center C.C.

The evolution from man to mankind is still in its infancy. Its main goal will be global cooperation and a total ban of wars. I do hope, the coming millennium will bring us closer to this destination.

Photo by Max-Planck-Institut

One of the nation's preeminent biologists, Edmond Fischer helped prove the importance of metabolism and cellular chemical reactions. After a forty-year tenure at the University of Washington, Fischer received the 1992 Nobel Prize for Physiology/Medicine.

Birthplace:
Shanghai, China

Age at the
Millennium: 80

DR. EDMOND H. FISCHER

United Nations   Nations Unies
NEW YORK   GENÈVE

In the biomedical sciences - which is my field - planning what will happen in even one hundred years is like asking a Cavalry General during the Civil War to plan for World War III. Nonetheless, I believe we will:

* Find life elsewhere in the Universe, colonize some planets.
* Master gene therapy to conquer genetic and other diseases.
* Learn how to regenerate nerves to overcome many forms of paralysis.
* Perhaps describe in molecular terms the mechanism of thought, memory and consciousness; prove scientifically that thought transmission really exists and show how it works.

Edmond H. Fischer
Nobel Laureate in Medicine or Physiology (1992)
signed in Seattle, Washington
May, 1997

©
UNITED
NATIONS

DR. CHARLES H. TOWNES

Birthplace:
Greenville, S.C.

**Age at the
Millennium: 85**

A scientist at Lucent Technologies' Bell Laboratories, Columbia, and MIT, Charles Townes developed maser and laser technologies. He received the 1964 Nobel Prize for Physics, accepting at the same ceremony as Martin Luther King.

United Nations   Nations Unies
NEW YORK   GENÈVE

Science will provide humans with
fantastic potentials. They can live
long; they can make the moon, ~~and~~
Mars, and Venus attractive living
places.
   What actually happens will
depend on the sense of values
society maintains, for example
how devoted individuals are to
the welfare of neighbors, descendents,
and our Earth.

Chas. H. Townes
(Charles H. Townes)
enroute Baltimore to San
Francisco April 30, 1997

Address

© UNITED NATIONS

Science will provide humans with fantastic potentials. They can live long; they can make the moon, Mars, and Venus attractive living places. What actually happens will depend on the sense of values society maintains, for example how devoted individuals are to the welfare of neighbors, descendants, and our Earth.

A molecular biologist at MIT who declined the university's presidency in 1990, Phillip Sharp received the 1993 Nobel Prize for Physiology/Medicine for his codiscovery of split genes, proof that DNA is not continuous, as previously believed.

Birthplace: Falmouth, Ky.

Age at the Millennium: 56

DR. PHILLIP A. SHARP

United Nations   Nations Unies
NEW YORK   GENÈVE

The beginning of the next millennium will be a time of great change, conflicts will be common. The mid part of the millennium will see the return of populations to more intellectual and less materialistic life styles. Throughout the millennium, science and new technologies will be the primary source of new wealth and power. Biology will be the prime new science of the next millennium and its discoveries will change us.

Address

Phillip A. Sharp, Salvador E. Luria Professor and Head of the Department of Biology

© UNITED NATIONS

Photo by Donna Coveney

DR. SIDNEY ALTMAN

Birthplace:
Montreal, Canada

**Age at the
Millennium: 61**

A biochemist at Yale since 1971, Sidney Altman made a major breakthrough in genetics by proving that the RNA molecule could rearrange itself. He received the Nobel Prize for Chemistry in 1989.

United Nations   Nations Unies
NEW YORK   GENÈVE

1. We will become more and more concerned with the environment.

2. Computers will become a more important part of our lives in ways we cannot imagine at the moment.

3. Our understanding of the brain will advance considerably and reveal some aspects of how "cognition" and "awareness" originate.

4. None of the above if there is widespread war.

Sidney Altman

Address

©
UNITED
NATIONS

1. *We will become more and more concerned with the environment.*

2. *Computers will become a more important part of our lives in ways we cannot imagine at the moment.*

3. *Our understanding of the brain will advance considerably and reveal some aspects of how "cognition" and "awareness" originate.*

4. *None of the above if there is widespread war.*

Photo by Michael Marsland

A survivor of Auschwitz, Elie Wiesel wrote extensively on the death of his family and became the world's foremost spokesman on the Holocaust. His works include *Night* and *Dawn*. In 1986 he received the Nobel Peace Prize.

**Birthplace:
Sighet, Romania**

**Age at the
Millennium: 72**

ELIE WIESEL

less fanaticism. More compassion for children. More solidarity with victims of illness and injustice —

Elie Wiesel

Less fanaticism. More compassion for children. More solidarity with victims of illness and injustice.

Photo by Nancy Rica Schiff / Saga / Archive Photos

DR. HARTMUT MICHEL

Birthplace:
Ludwigsburg, Germany

Age at the Millennium: 52

An accomplished biochemist, Hartmut Michel had a key role in identifying the three-dimensional structure of photosynthesis—the most important chemical reaction on Earth. Michel received the 1988 Nobel Prize for Chemistry with codiscoverer Robert Huber.

Prediction: The fossil fuel will be largely consumed. As a result the climate will be warm and humid. Gasoline and transport will be prohibitively expensive. The population will reach 20 Billion. An incredible wealth of information exists.

Hope: Caused by a better education population growth can be stopped at 8 Billion. Only renewable energy sources are used. Knowledge is used for the benefit of all human beings only!

Address

Frankfurt/Main, Germany
20-01-98

© UNITED NATIONS

Prediction: The fossil fuel will be largely consumed. As a result the climate will be warm and humid. Gasoline and transport will be prohibitively expensive. The population will reach 20 Billion. An incredible wealth of information exists.

Hope: Caused by a better education population growth can be stopped at 8 Billion. Only renewable energy sources are used. Knowledge is used for the benefit of all human beings only!

A chemist who emigrated from Hungary in the 1950s, George Olah has had tremendous success in the area of new fuel development. For his breakthrough in stabilizing hydrocarbons and the study of their chemical reactions, Olah received the 1994 Nobel Prize for Chemistry.

Birthplace:
Budapest, Hungary

Age at the Millennium: 73

DR. GEORGE A. OLAH

Science will continue in the 21st Century to widen our knowledge hopefully for the benefit of mankind and to make the world better for future generations

GEORGE A. OLAH
1994 NOBEL LAUREATE IN CHEMISTRY

Address

© UNITED NATIONS

Science will continue in the 21st Century to widen our knowledge hopefully for the benefit of mankind and to make the world better for future generations.

DR. JOHN POLANYI

Birthplace:
Berlin, Germany

Age at the Millennium: 71

A renowned chemist with the University of Toronto, John Polanyi was the first to record the spectrum of hydrogen gas being broken into single atoms. For this breakthrough in understanding chemical reactions, Polanyi received the 1986 Nobel Prize for Chemistry.

United Nations   **Nations Unies**
NEW YORK   GENÈVE

Toronto, Canada, Feb. 28, 1998.

My hope for the coming millennium is also my prediction: The nations of the world will come to realise that anarchy is even less acceptable on the world scene than in one's neighbourhood. We shall therefore build a system of world law, and in the process abolish war.

John Polanyi

UNITED
NATIONS

My hope for the coming millennium is also my prediction: The nations of the world will come to realize that anarchy is even less acceptable on the world scene than in one's neighborhood. We shall therefore build a system of world law, and in the process abolish war.

A geneticist at the National Institutes of Health and University of Texas, Joseph Goldstein partnered with Michael Brown to identify the metabolism of cholesterol deficiencies in heart disease. Goldstein received the 1985 Nobel Prize for Physiology/Medicine.

Birthplace:
Sumter, S.C.

Age at the Millennium: 60

DR. JOSEPH L. GOLDSTEIN

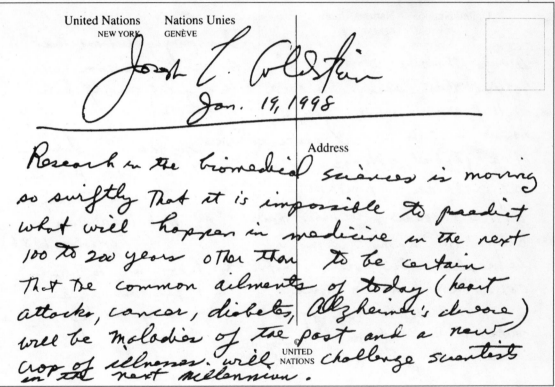

United Nations   Nations Unies
NEW YORK   GENÈVE

Joseph L. Goldstein

Jan. 19, 1998

Address

Research in the biomedical sciences is moving so swiftly That it is impossible to predict what will happen in medicine in the next 100 to 200 years other than to be certain That the common ailments of today (heart attacks, cancer, diabetes, Alzheimer's disease) will be maladies of the past and a new crop of illnesses will challenge scientists in the next millennium.

UNITED NATIONS

Research in the biomedical sciences is moving so swiftly that it is impossible to predict what will happen in medicine in the next 100 to 200 years other than to be certain that the common ailments of today (heart attacks, cancer, diabetes, Alzheimer's disease) will be maladies of the past and a new crop of illnesses will challenge scientists in the next millennium.

Photo by Photo Gittings

DR. YUAN T. LEE

Birthplace:
Hsinchu, Republic
of China

Age at the
Millennium: 64

A chemist at the University of California most of his career, Yuan Lee created an apparatus that greatly advanced the ability to identify the dynamics of molecular chemical processes. Lee received the 1986 Nobel Prize for Chemistry.

United Nations   Nations Unies
NEW YORK   GENÈVE

During the next century, I believe that everyone on earth will learn to work together as an unit in a true sense of a "global village". Not only military confrontations will disappear, blind economical competition among nations will be replaced by more meaningful collaboration as we move into a borderless society, to maintain a sustainable development of the entire world.

© UNITED NATIONS

I strongly believe that the next millenium will be a great turning point of mankind.

Address

Yuan T. Lee *
President, Academia Sinica, Taiwan ROC.
Nobel Laureate
(Chemistry, 1986.)

* I returned to Taiwan in 1994, and became a citizen of the Republic of China.

During the next century, I believe that everyone on earth will learn to work together as an unit in a true sense of a "global village." Not only military confrontations will disappear, blind economical competition among nations will be replaced by more meaningful collaboration as we move into a borderless society, to maintain a sustainable development of the entire world. I strongly believe that the next millennium will be a great turning point of mankind.

Canada's greatest biochemist, Michael Smith has contributed to the corporate and academic advancements of the biotechnology industry. His advances in protein structure analysis earned him the 1993 Nobel Prize for Chemistry.

Birthplace:
Blackpool, England

Age at the Millennium: 68

DR. MICHAEL SMITH

United Nations   Nations Unies
NEW YORK   GENÈVE

I am a scientist, and therefore sceptical of the value of predictions about the future. What I can do is make a wish for the next millennium — a wish that the human race soon learns to live in harmony — in harmony with fellow humans, in harmony with the biological world and in harmony with the physical world

Michael Smith

UNITED NATIONS

MAY 1, 1997 - VANCOUVER, CANADA

I am a scientist, and therefore skeptical of the value of predictions about the future. What I can do is make a wish for the next millennium—a wish that the human race soon learns to live in harmony—in harmony with fellow humans, in harmony with the biological world and in harmony with the physical world.

DR. STEVEN CHU

Birthplace:
Saint Louis, Mo.

Age at the
Millennium: 52

The former director of the Quantum Electronics Department of Lucent Technologies' Bell Labs, Steven Chu joined the staff of Stanford University in 1987. Chu received the 1997 Nobel Prize for Physics for his advancements in laser spectroscopy.

United Nations   Nations Unies
NEW YORK   GENÈVE

Address

My hope is that we will attain a new level of harmony between ourselves and our planet.

Stanford January 31, 1998

©
UNITED
NATIONS

My hope is that we will attain a new level of harmony between ourselves and our planet.

7   A brilliant economist at Harvard, Kenneth Arrow created the "impossibility theorem" and also contributed to the definition of popular equilibrium. Arrow was awarded the Nobel Prize for Economics in 1972.

Birthplace:
New York, N.Y.

Age at the Millennium: 79

DR. KENNETH J. ARROW

United Nations   **Nations Unies**
NEW YORK   GENÈVE

The world of the year 3,000 will be unimaginable in many ways. Let me just pick one development — the great reduction in energy useage (by greater efficiency) and the end of dependence on carbon-based fuels. The global warming problem and air pollution will disappear.

Kenneth J. Arrow

KENNETH J. ARROW

Address

©
UNITED
NATIONS

The world of the year 3,000 will be unimaginable in many ways. Let me just pick one development—the great reduction in energy usage (by greater efficiency) and the end of dependence on carbon-based fuels. The global warming problem and air pollution will disappear.

DR. CHRISTIAN B. ANFINSEN

Birthplace: Monesson, Pa.

Deceased 1997

Christian Anfinsen made a breakthrough in understanding the function of amino acids for which he was awarded the 1972 Nobel Prize for Chemistry. Dr. Anfinsen passed away in 1997 at age 80.

United Nations   Nations Unies
NEW YORK   GENÈVE

בס״ד
14 Iyar 5757

"Whatever you can do, or dream you can, Begin it !! Boldness has genius, power and magic in it !!"
May 1995/1997
Baltimore, Maryland

צדוק
מבורות

Libby Anfinsen / Christian Boehmer Anfinsen

Address

WIDOW OF
PROF. CHRISTIAN B. ANFINSEN

©
UNITED NATIONS

"Whatever you can do, or dream you can, Begin it!! Boldness has genius, power and magic in it!!"

(From Mrs. Libby Anfinsen:"The selection of the quote contributed is one which my husband carried in his wallet. Rather than of predictive value, it is one of the yardsticks he used in conducting, so beautifully, the intricate symphony that was his life. He advocated human respect, and indeed, represented humanity at its very best.")

A Harvard physicist with over thirty years tenure, the Dutch-born Nicolaas Bloembergen developed the first continuous high-intensity laser. Bloembergen received the National Medal of Science Award and in 1981 was awarded the Nobel Prize for Physics.

Birthplace: Dordrecht, Netherlands

Age at the Millennium: 80

DR. NICOLAAS BLOEMBERGEN

United Nations Nations Unies
NEW YORK **GENÈVE**

I hope and expect that men and women everywhere will place more emphasis on the quality rather than the quantity of human life. Fewer people than exist on the earth today could lead a more prosperous and more peaceful life in the year 3000.

Nicolaas Bloembergen

Cambridge, MA, USA, 1 May 1997

© UNITED NATIONS

I hope and expect that men and women everywhere will place more emphasis on the quality rather than the quantity of human life. Fewer people than exist on the earth today could lead a more prosperous and more peaceful life in the year 3000.

Photo by John Kennard

DR. DOUGLAS D. OSHEROFF

Birthplace:
Aberdeen, Wash.

Age at the
Millennium: 55

A leading American physicist, Douglas Osheroff has made numerous breakthroughs in identifying the properties of matter in solid and low temperature states. For his many discoveries, including 3He superfluidity, Osheroff received the 1996 Nobel Prize for Physics.

United Nations   Nations Unies
NEW YORK   GENÈVE

Civilization will convert to a hydrogen based energy economy to avoid the pollution of our atmosphere. Hydrogen will be derived from fossil fuels until these hydrocarbons become vastly more useful as raw materials for manufacturing. Ultimately, hydrogen will be separated from water using solar energy as a power source.

If man does not learn to control population growth by more benign means, disease and famine will limit the human population to roughly twelve billion persons.

Address

January 13, 1998
Douglas D. Osheroff

©
UNITED
NATIONS

One of the greatest minds of molecular biology, Kary Mullis devised methods for better examining DNA and multiplying its fragments (the basis for Michael Crichton's novel *Jurassic Park*). Mullis received the 1993 Nobel Prize for Chemistry.

Birthplace:
Lenoir, N.C.

Age at the Millennium: 56

DR. KARY B. MULLIS

United Nations   Nations Unies
NEW YORK   GENÈVE

The only prediction which I think is of significance to humans and which will be accurate for the interval 2001-3000 AD is that the Sun will rise once every day everywhere except for the poles. It will happen .ca. 365.24... x 10^3 times.

Address

Kary B Mullis

Dr. Kary B. Mullis
La Jolla, California   1997

©
UNITED
NATIONS

DR. BARUCH S. BLUMBERG

Birthplace:
New York, N.Y.

Age at the Millennium: 75

The chief biochemist of the Fox Chase Cancer Center, Baruch Blumberg discovered the antigen that made screening for hepatitis B possible. For this and other breakthroughs Blumberg received the 1976 Nobel Prize for Physiology/Medicine.

United Nations   **Nations Unies**
NEW YORK   GENÈVE

MILLENIUM COMMITTEE OF NEW YORK

Box 20292 Dag Hammarskjold Center C.C., New York, NY 10017

Biological and medical research during the next few decades will increase our understanding of why some people become ill and others do not. There will be greater knowledge of the genes that increase and decrease susceptibility to infectious agents, other pathogenic agents in the environment and of the interaction of the persons own genome with these external agents. This will allow individualization of health maintenance so that each person can be aware of their own susceptibility and resistance and, in a balanced manner, manage their lives to avoid hazard. It will also be possible to predict which patient will respond to a particular drug and who will not. Treatment will be individualized. The hope is that people will live somewhat longer and that their lives will be healthier, even in old age. It is difficult to predict if this wisdom will be used for the overall betterment of humankind, but, as I am an optimist, I believe it will.

Because of the greater awareness of the environment there will be an increasing need to understand and live in harmony with our natural world. This will require a better interaction of the problem-solving capabilities of science and the irrational sensitivities of humans. This too, I believe, will happen, but who will be able to perceive it?

Baruch S. Blumberg, Fox Chase Cancer Center, Philadelphia, PA, USA, June 1997

Baruch S. Blumberg,   *aug 1997*

The exiled leader of Tibet, the Dalai Lama won the 1989 Nobel Peace Prize for pursuing the nonviolent independence of his country. A holy prophet to Tibetans since 1937, the Dalai Lama has become revered by millions worldwide.

Birthplace:
Takster, China

Age at the
Millennium: 65

THE DALAI LAMA

United Nations   Nations Unies
NEW YORK   GENÈVE

```
As a result of the experiences
that mankind has gone through
in the 20th century it is my
view that we will act with
more maturity in the next
century and thus create
better prospects for peace,
harmony and tolerance.
```

Address

©
UNITED
NATIONS

Photo by Monitor / Archive Photos

DR. LEON M. LEDERMAN

Birthplace:
New York, N.Y.

Age at the Millennium: 78

A physicist at Columbia University, Leon Lederman discovered the subatomic particle muon neutrino. In 1979 he became director of the Fermi National Laboratory in Chicago and was awarded the Nobel Prize for Physics in 1988.

United Nations Nations Unies
NEW YORK GENÈVE

I have two choices for the next millenium: one optimistic, one not. Both project technology in a plausible way. In the bleak view greed and fear continue to dominate human behavior. An elite group, suitably secured, will employ a complex helmet to provide "virtual satisfaction" via adjustable voltages and currents to the satisfaction centers of the brain. These simulate precisely the pleasures of food, success, sex, sports, professional success, adulation, pain, whatever! Robots and servants look to the needs of the ever-smiling users. In the bright view, Technology becomes a servant of all the people. Population is stablized, the new sources of energy encourages environmental remediation. Clean, efficient nano-technologies manufacture, from molecular modules, all the needs of the planet. War, disease, drugs are obsolete. There is no cash. Transactions are via DNA authenticated credit devices. Taxes are automatically subtracted. And a growing number of citizens are signing up for the virtual satisfaction helmets.

UNITED NATIONS

CHICAGO, MAY '97

Leon M. Lederman

I have two choices for the next millennium: one optimistic, one not. Both project technology in a plausible way. In the bleak view greed and fear continue to dominate human behavior. An elite group, suitably secured, will employ a complex helmet to provide "virtual satisfaction" via adjustable voltages and currents to the satisfaction centers of the brain. These simulate precisely the pleasures of food, sex, sports, professional success, adulation, pain, whatever! Robots and servants look to the needs of the ever-smiling users. In the bright view, technology becomes a servant of all the people.

Population is stabilized, the new sources of energy encourages environmental remediation. Clean, efficient nano-technologies manufacture, from molecular modules, all the needs of the planet. War, disease, drugs are obsolete. There is no cash. Transactions are via DNA authenticated credit devices. Taxes are automatically subtracted. And a growing number of citizens are signing up for the virtual satisfaction helmets.

Photo by Fermilab Visual Media Services

Chapter 3

American Government

CHRISTINE TODD WHITMAN

Birthplace:
Tewksbury, N.J.

Age at the Millennium: 54

The governor of New Jersey, Christine Todd Whitman has become one of the most prominent Republicans in the country since her unexpected election in 1993. Seen as a highly effective administrator, Whitman is often touted as a presidential running mate.

United Nations   Nations Unies
NEW YORK   GENEVE

Message for the Third Millennium:

We've seen throughout the world that democracy works, that education pays off, that intolerance destroys, and that free markets expand opportunity. And on every continent, a commitment to careful stewardship of the world's precious resources is reawakening.

Address

My hope for the future is that we continue to follow the path of progress and prosperity.

Christine Todd Whitman
Governor of New Jersey
Trenton, N.J.   1998

UNITED
NATIONS

A congressman from 1984 to 1993, Leon Panetta was chosen by President Bill Clinton as his chief of staff. Panetta served until the end of Clinton's first term, and is credited with making many improvements to that administration's structure and agenda.

**Birthplace:
Monterey, Calif.**

**Age at the
Millennium: 54**

LEON E. PANETTA

United Nations · Nations Unies
NEW YORK · GENÈVE

Address

© UNITED NATIONS

My Italian parents immigrated to America in the 1930s because they wanted a better life for their children. They fulfilled that dream. I want the same dream for my children and the children of all the world. My prediction is that in the next millennium, no child will go to bed hungry—and every child will have a better life than his or her parents.

RUTH BADER GINSBURG

Birthplace:
New York, N.Y.

Age at the Millennium: 67

The second woman named to the U.S. Supreme Court, Ruth Bader Ginsburg was President Clinton's first Supreme Court appointment. The quality of Ginsburg's legal opinions have made her one of the Supreme Court's most popular jurists.

United Nations   Nations Unies
NEW YORK   GENÈVE

My hope for the next millennium is that the motto, E Pluribus Unum (of many, one), will become a reality for the people of the United States and of the world.

Ruth Bader Ginsburg

Ruth Bader Ginsburg
Associate Justice
Supreme Court of the
    United States
April 28, 1997
Washington, D.C., USA

Address

©
UNITED
NATIONS

Secretary of Defense under Presidents Kennedy and Johnson, McNamara oversaw U.S. military policy in Vietnam from 1961 to 1967, ultimately resigning over the war's direction. McNamara was also president of Ford Motor Company and the World Bank.

Birthplace:
San Francisco, Calif.

Age at the Millennium: 84

ROBERT S. MCNAMARA

United Nations
NEW YORK

Nations Unies
GENÈVE

1/v 0/98

I believe that the indefinite combination of human fallibility and nuclear weapons will lead to destruction of nations. Therefore, I predict the next millennium will witness either nuclear catastrophe or the elimination of nuclear weapons. We must act now to ensure it is the latter.

Robert S. McNamara
Washington, D.C. — USA

© UNITED NATIONS

Address

I believe that the indefinite combination of human fallibility and nuclear weapons will lead to destruction of nations. Therefore, I predict the next millennium will witness either nuclear catastrophe or the elimination of nuclear weapons. We must act now to ensure it is the latter.

NEWT GINGRICH

Birthplace:
Harrisburg, Pa.

Age at the
Millennium: 57

Speaker of the House of Representatives since 1995, Newt Gingrich has led an historic conservative agenda through Congress. His victorious "Contract with America" made him *Time*'s 1996 "Man of the Year" and the unofficial leader of the Republican Party.

United Nations   Nations Unies
NEW YORK   GENÈVE

The First settlements beyond our galaxy will have occurred by 2500 we will have left the solar system by 2200. We will have permanent colonies on Moon, Mars and asteroids by 2100

Newt Dgit

Address Speaker
U S House
Washington DC

©
UNITED
NATIONS

The first settlements beyond our galaxy will have occurred by 2500. We will have left the solar system by 2200. We will have permanent colonies on Moon, Mars and asteriods by 2100.

Secretary of Labor during President Clinton's entire first term, Robert Reich has also written several books on neoliberal economics, which he taught at Yale. In his youth, Reich attended Oxford University with Clinton as a fellow Rhodes scholar.

Birthplace:
Scranton, Pa.

Age at the
Millennium: 54

ROBERT B. REICH

United Nations   Nations Unies
NEW YORK   GENÈVE

The first century of the third millennium will be one of extraordinary peace o prosperity for much of the world, and it will be accompanied by a great flowering of art, literature, o advances in human health o well being. The real trouble will start in the first third of the third century of the third millennium. I do not plan to be there.

RmmB.Reich
Cambridge, MA.   January 7, 1998

The first century of the third millennium will be one of extraordinary peace and prosperity for much of the world, and it will be accompanied by a great flowering of art, literature, and advances in human health and well being. The real trouble will start in the first third of the third century of the third millennium. I do not plan to be there.

SHIRLEY CHISHOLM

Birthplace:
New York, N.Y.

Age at the Millennium: 76

The first African American congresswoman in the United States, Shirley Chisholm represented her New York district for fourteen years. An articulate defender of civil rights, Chisholm pursued the presidency in the 1972 Democratic primaries before retiring.

United Nations   Nations Unies
NEW YORK   GENÈVE

It is my belief that Man will walk in space and that more attention will be given to that planet above the planet Earth!

Address

Shirley Chisholm

Palm Coast, Florida

©
UNITED
NATIONS

It is my belief that Man will walk in space and that more attention will be given to that planet above the planet Earth!

Photo by Archive Photos

As White House Press Secretary under Presidents Reagan and Bush, Marlin Fitzwater fielded media issues from Iran Contra to Desert Storm. Fitzwater remains in Washington and frequently comments on current media issues.

Birthplace:
Salina, Kans.

Age at the
Millennium: 58

MARLIN FITZWATER

United Nations · Nations Unies
NEW YORK · GENÈVE

Religion will become the central political face in America, possessing the only idealism strong enough to realign political parties and hold broad coalitions together.

Address

Marlin Fitzwater

June 2, 1997

Washington D.C.

© UNITED NATIONS

Religion will become the central political force in America, possessing the only idealism strong enough to realign political parties and hold broad coalitions together.

Photo by Howard Sachs / CNP / Archive Photos

JOHN B. ANDERSON

Birthplace: Rockford, Ill.

Age at the Millennium: 78

A presidential candidate in the 1980 election, John Anderson made headlines when he ran as a third-party independent against President Carter and Ronald Reagan. Anderson had been a Republican congressman for eighteen years before his candidacy.

United Nations · Nations Unies
NEW YORK · GENÈVE

My prediction for the next millennium is that the cardinal principle of world peace through world law will be implemented in progressive stages beginning with an International Criminal Court which in a few years into the 21st Century will be joined by an International Peace-Keeping and Peace-Making Force as a strong and effective agency of an empowered, restructured UN which will gradually take shape as a democratic world federation.

Address

John B Anderson

Fort Lauderdale, FL.

U. S. A.

August 23, 1997

© UNITED NATIONS

The first female governor of Texas, Ann Richards became one of the nation's most powerful Democrats—even delivering the keynote address at the Democratic National Convention. In 1994 Richards lost unexpectedly to George W. Bush.

Birthplace:
Lakeview, Tex.

Age at the Millennium: 67

ANN RICHARDS

United Nations   Nations Unies
NEW YORK   GENÈVE

Women will be the majority of the heads of state of nations and Secretary general of the U.N.

Ann Richards

Address

A. Richards former governor of Texas.
April 30, 1997
Austin, Texas
USA.

UNITED NATIONS

Women will be the majority of the heads of state of nations and secretary general of the U.N.

GEN. H. NORMAN SCHWARZKOPF

Birthplace:
Trenton, N.J.

Age at the Millennium: 66

Given command of the fifty-six-nation coalition force in Operation Desert Storm, General H. Norman Schwarzkopf oversaw the liberation of Kuwait and the destruction of Iraq's Republican Guard. In 1992 Schwarzkopf was appointed a five-star general.

United Nations   Nations Unies
NEW YORK   GENÈVE

World Peace !

Address

5/20/97   *TAMPA FL.*

©
UNITED
NATIONS

World Peace!

One of the most prominent personalities in American politics, Mario Cuomo served as governor of New York from 1983 to 1995. An articulate spokesman for the Democratic Party and liberalism, Cuomo has long been urged to run for president.

Birthplace:
New York, N.Y.

Age at the Millennium: 68

MARIO CUOMO

United Nations   Nations Unies
NEW YORK   GENÈVE

Predictions for the Next Millennium:

The interconnectedness and interdependence of nations will become more-and-more obvious. And it will spur more-and-more linkages and mergers of political powers. The European community economy, 350 million strong, will be well-established and successful. The Euro and the Dollar will dominate a bi-polar economy, sharing dominance. We will have to work out ranges and target zones for the values of the two currencies to avoid de-stabilization. The United States - having gone through a late Twentieth Century devolution phase, in which it sought to dispense national functions to the states thereby fragmenting the national power - will reverse course and increase its nationalism in order to compete with the united forces of the European community and analogous mergers in the East.

MARIO CUOMO
New York City, 1998

Provided to the Millennium Committee of New York LLC in commemoration of the arrival of the Third Millennium.

©
UNITED
NATIONS

RODNEY FRELINGHUYSEN

Birthplace:
New York, N.Y.

**Age at the
Millennium:** 54

A Republican congressman from New Jersey, Rodney Frelinghuysen's family has been active in American politics since the Revolutionary War. In the House, Frelinghuysen has advanced lower tax rates, veterans' rights, and the preservation of open spaces.

98

United Nations   Nations Unies
NEW YORK   GENÈVE

Largely due to our investment in funding the National Institute of Health we will eradicate cancer for men, women & children.

Rodney Frelinghuysen
M.C. (New Jersey)

Address

©
UNITED
NATIONS

Largely due to our investment in funding the National Institutes of Health we will eradicate cancer for men, women and children.

America's most famous Surgeon General, C. Everett Koop was appointed to the public health position by President Reagan, serving from 1981 to 1989. Koop greatly advanced the public's knowledge on the risks from AIDS and smoking.

Birthplace:
New York, N.Y.

Age at the Millennium: 84

DR. C. EVERETT KOOP

United Nations
NEW YORK

Nations Unies
GENÈVE

During the early years of the next millenium, blood transfusion as we know it will be gradually replaced by a substitute-a hemoglobin-based oxygen carrier, which for many indications is better than blood.

©
UNITED
NATIONS

OLIVER NORTH

Birthplace:
San Antonio, Tex.

Age at the Millennium: 57

A decorated Vietnam veteran in the Marine Corps, Oliver North became famous for his role in the Iran Contra scandal while serving on President Reagan's staff. Given a suspended sentence, North later ran for the U.S. Senate.

United Nations   Nations Unies
NEW YORK   GENÈVE

That all people will be free!

Address

©
UNITED
NATIONS

That all people will be free!

Photo by Audia

The former chief of the LAPD, Daryl Gates served as an adviser to presidents and government agencies on crime prevention. Gates developed the first SWAT team and pioneered the use of helicopters by police.

Birthplace:
Glendale, Calif.

Age at the Millennium: 74

DARYL F. GATES

DARYL F. GATES June 11, 1997
CHIEF Los Angeles Police Dept.

I believe the next century will bring peace to the streets of our cities in America. Crime and violence will be reduced significantly. Narcotic and alcohol addiction will be erased by scientific discovery. The sharp differences between ethnicity and class will be narrowed—If this does not happen it will make no difference—we will cease to exist.

Photo by Reuters/Lee Celano/Archive Photos

DONALD RUMSFELD

Birthplace:
Chicago, Ill.

Age at the Millennium: 68

A former secretary of both Treasury and Defense, Donald Rumsfeld served in the cabinets of Presidents Nixon and Ford from 1969 to 1977. Rumsfeld was also Ford's chief of staff, ambassador to NATO, and later the CEO of General Instrument Corp.

United Nations   Nations Unies
NEW YORK   GENÈVE

January 6, 1998
Chicago, Illinois
USA
Predictions for the 21st Century

- The 1st Quarter of the 21st Century has the potential to be a period of unprecedented economic growth.

- Mankind will likely learn more about the human brain in the 1st half of the 21st Century than we have learned in preceding centuries.

- Not withstanding the end of the Cold War, our planet has not been magically transformed into a modern day Eden. The lesson that our generations learned from hard experience is that weakness is provocative. Every other generation seems to have to relearn that lesson.

- To paraphrase Theodore Roosevelt, "aggressive fighting for the right will continue to be the noblest sport the world affords."

Donald Rumsfeld

Address

© NITED .TIONS

A three-term U.S. senator from Ohio, Howard Metzenbaum first entered politics in 1943. After elected to the Senate in 1976, Metzenbaum rose through the Democratic Party ranks to become one of Washington's most powerful legislators.

Birthplace:
Cleveland, Ohio

Age at the
Millennium: 83

HOWARD M. METZENBAUM

United Nations · Nations Unies
NEW YORK · GENÈVE

A cure for cancer and AIDS will be found. Autos will operate on agricultural products as fuel. There will be auto-free communities with people movers. Unfortunately racial and religious bars will continue to exist. More non-whites will become international (and national) economic, political and scientific leaders. Regrettably, the have-nots of the world will not improve much. There will be a devastating destructive war far worse than anything experienced to date.

PHILIP N. DIEHL

Birthplace:
Dallas, Tex.

Age at the Millennium: 56

As the director of the U. S. Mint, Philip Diehl oversees the printing of the nation's coins (20 billion annually) and the protection of the nation's $100 billion in gold and silver reserves (including Fort Knox).

Washington, D.C. July 4, 1997
The United States of America

Greetings from your ancestors--

Mankind expected the world to end when the first millennium ended. At the end of the second millennium, we believe you will stand on our shoulders to reach what we could not and to see what we nearly saw. We want you to know we thought of you, envied you, and wanted the best for you. We tried to leave you the best world we could, for we knew that part of us would be in each of you. We wish you good luck.

Philip N. Diehl
Director
United States Mint

The only person to have challenged Ross Perot for the presidential nomination of Perot's own Reform Party, Richard Lamm was a popular three-term governor of Colorado from 1975 to 1987. Now a professor, Lamm is a respected expert on public policy.

Birthplace:
Madison, Wis.

Age at the Millennium: 65

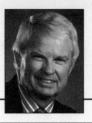

RICHARD D. LAMM

United Nations Nations Unies
NEW YORK GENÈVE

"*Age*" will be as large an issue in the next 40 years, as race has been in the last 40 years.

Address

We shall soon have to run a nation of 50 Floridas with social systems that are demographically obsolete. It will not be politics as usual.

Jan, 1998
Denver, Colorado

©
UNITED
NATIONS

"Age" will be as large an issue in the next 40 years, as race has been in the last 40 years.

We shall soon have to run a nation of 50 Floridas with social systems that are demographically obsolete. It will not be politics as usual.

Photo by Berkeley

ADMIRAL ELMO R. ZUMWALT JR.

Birthplace:
San Francisco, Calif.

Age at the Millennium: 80

A key arms strategist advising the White House during the Cuban Missile Crisis, Elmo Zumwalt would be made chief of Naval Operations during the Vietnam War under President Nixon. He retired in 1974 to enter private enterprise.

United Nations   Nations Unies
NEW YORK   GENÈVE

During the next millennium the world will experience and recover from terrorist inspired biological, chemical, and nuclear attacks on cities. These tragedies, and the increasingly interlocked global economy will have led to a system of confederated world states with an effective and functioning world federation.

Mankind will have eliminated disease and hunger. The work week will consist of 3 days. Lives will last for an average of 150 years.

Arlington, Virginia, June 4, 1997

Elmo R Zumwalt J
Admiral USN Retired

© UNITED NATIONS

During the next millennium the world will experience and recover from terrorist inspired biological, chemical, and nuclear attacks on cities. These tragedies, and the increasingly interlocked global economy will have led to a system of confederated world states with an effective and functioning world federation.

Mankind will have eliminated disease and hunger. The work week will consist of 3 days. Lives will last for an average of 150 years.

When Captain Scott O'Grady's F-16 was shot down over Bosnia in 1995, he survived undetected in a forest for six days before making radio contact and being rescued. He received a hero's welcome in the United States.

Birthplace:
Indianapolis, Ind.

Age at the Millennium: 34

CAPT. SCOTT O'GRADY

United Nations   Nations Unies

NEW YORK   GENÈVE

In the next Millennium I predict that the U.S. will have it's first female president!

Address

©
UNITED
NATIONS

In the next millennium I predict that the U.S. will have its first female president!

ALEXIS M. HERMAN

Birthplace:
Mobile, Ala.

Age at the Millennium: 53

The current U.S. secretary of labor, Alexis Herman is the first African American to head the department. Seen as a rising star in Washington, Herman received bipartisan support for her nomination and was widely praised for her role in the UPS and GM strike settlements.

United Nations   Nations Unies
NEW YORK   GENÈVE

My hope for the future is for a world where all work is honored and all workers are prized. It is for a place where every child can grow to their God-given potential--and every adult has the opportunity to achieve. But we don't have to wait until the next millennium to see that future materialize. We can start today--because the answer is in the human heart. That is our task.

Alexis M. Herman

Address

©
UNITED
NATIONS

The chairman of the Federal Reserve Board prior to Alan Greenspan, Paul Volcker oversaw U.S. monetary policy from 1979 to 1987, enduring the economic cycles of both the Carter and Reagan administrations. He now teaches at Princeton University.

Birthplace:
Cape May, N.J.

Age at the Millennium: 73

PAUL VOLCKER

United Nations   Nations Unies
NEW YORK   GENÈVE

Long before the year 3,000, national currencies will largely disappear—and sometime thereafter the nation/state as we know it. Meanwhile, there is a large potential for political turbulence and conflict—but it will be kept in bounds by our obvious interdependence—economically, environmentally, and socially.

Paul Volcker

©
UNITED
NATIONS

Long before the year 3,000, national currencies will largely disappear—and sometime thereafter the nation/state as we know it. Meanwhile, there is a large potential for political turbulence and conflict

—but it will be kept in bounds by our obvious interdependence—economically, environmentally, and socially.

STEPHEN BREYER

Birthplace:
San Francisco, Calif.

**Age at the
Millennium:** 62

Confirmed to the U. S. Supreme Court in 1994, Stephen Breyer received strong bi-partisan support from Congress. Prior to this assignment, Breyer had taught at Harvard and served as a circuit court judge.

United Nations   Nations Unies
NEW YORK   GENÈVE

6/24/97

My prediction, and certainly my hope, for the year 3000 is that the year will see one more of a series of democratic elections for President of the United States -- held regularly at four year intervals, as in the past; and I hope by then, too, a rule of law, providing similarly fair, democratic procedures and protecting basic human liberties, will extend to every part of the globe.

Washington, D.C.   1997

©
UNITED
NATIONS

Stephen Breyer

My prediction, and certainly my hope, for the year 3000 is that the year will see one more of a series of democratic elections for President of the United States—held regularly at four year intervals, as in the past; and I hope by then, too, a rule of law, providing similarly fair, democratic procedures and protecting basic human liberties, will extend to every part of the globe.

Chapter 4

World Government

LORD JAMES CALLAGHAN

Birthplace:
Portsmouth, England

Age at the
Millennium: 88

When he became prime minister of the United Kingdom in 1976, Lord James Callaghan had already held numerous key cabinet posts in British Parliament. Succeeded by Margaret Thatcher, Callaghan was later made a baron in the House of Lords.

United Nations   Nations Unies
NEW YORK   GENÈVE

To 3000 AD.

Despite the 1000 years that separate us I am certain that the human heart will never cease to strive for love, for peace, for equality & justice for all the world's peoples. May you have found the answers that we still seek in hope, and in Freedom,

James Callaghan
Prime Minister, 1976-1979.

© UNITED NATIONS

To 3000 AD: Despite the 1000 years that separate us I am certain that the human heart will never cease to strive for love, for peace, for equality and justice for all the world's peoples. May you have found the answers that we still seek in hope, and in Freedom.

The first woman to lead a Muslim nation, Benazir Bhutto entered Pakistan's politics after years of house arrest. Easily elected prime minister in 1988, her role as a powerful Asian leader ended by 1997 when forced out of office.

**Birthplace:
Karachi, Pakistan**

**Age at the
Millennium: 47**

BENAZIR BHUTTO

MESSAGE FROM HER EXCELLENCY, FORMER PRIME MINISTER BENAZIR BHUTTO, ON THE THIRD MILLENNIUM: Predictions about the future are extraordinarily difficult. Surely at the end of the first millennium in 999, no sane woman or man could have predicted, the triumphs, tragedies and technologies of the emerging twentieth century. But based on the political, economic, informational, cultural and technological integration of our planet in the second half of the 20th century, there are extraordinary changes that I see ahead for mankind as we progress across the millennium and well into the next 1000 years.

First, I anticipate that the world will see an almost total integration of polities, economies and people into a truly global community. I envision the erosion of the concept of the nation-state as we move deeper in the millennium (the establishment of the World Trade Organization last year being the precursor of this era of internationalism.) Multi-nationals will replace nations as political and trading blocs, and an emerging world political structure will supersede nations as we currently know them. Just as a world government will develop dominated by multi-nationals, structures to regulate the worlds interrelated economies will emerge. The Federal Reserve will no longer dictate monetary policy for the United States, but a similar international organization will perform that same function for the integrated global economy (modeled, once again, after the World Trade Organization). The erosion of the concept of national sovereignty will cause the creation of local corporations taking on the task to preserve and protect security and social services in their local areas all over the world. Therefore powerful multinational corporations will soon emerge as extra-legal players in shaping the new millennium. Since markets are replacing missiles as the measure of might, those who control markets and commerce will be the source of real political power in the next millennium, and those entities are global multi-nationals whose allegiance is to open trade, open markets and high profits, and not to the provincial concerns of individual nations.

I also envision an increase in the importance of individuals and communities in the third millennium world order, corresponding to the weakening of nation-states. People will identify with their communities and with people like themselves all over the world. The Internet will provide an equal playing field for all of the world's children with respect to education, access and opportunity, and cybernetics will replace traditional classroom education as the instrument of social change in the emerging world society. However large segments of society which do not understand the tools of technology will be marginalised.

I see a third millennium where blocs of nations, and aggregations of interests emerge. The uni-polar world of Pan Americana will give way once again to a multi-polar world. In this multi-polar world, the Muslim community will exercise more influence than it does now. I see third millennium where a new spiritual awakening takes place. Material goods will no longer be enough to satisfy the inner cravings of an individual in a world where machines play an increasingly large role. I see a third millennium of new diseases, new methods of destruction, but new technological triumphs that dramatically increase the quality of life for the new millennium's people. I see life expectancy doubling over the third millennium, where it will someday be the case the people will live for as long as they wish, or more precisely for as long as they can afford to live.

I see an increasingly difficult moral dilemma in the new millennium over the question of cloning, which will ultimately lead to organ donor harvesting through ones own clones. I see a third millennium where travel to the moon, and the planets of this solar system becomes common place; where crops are harvested and resources are mined and even water is imported from the depths of space, as space travel becomes more cost efficient and much faster, and as the children of earth continue to despoil the ecology and environment of our planet, and deplete our planets natural resources.

In the early part of the new millennium, I envision that the oil and gas reserves of Central Asia will dramatically eclipse those of the Middle East and Persian Gulf, with a corresponding impact on not only the world's economy, but on the relative importance of Central Asia vis a vis the Gulf in the third millennium political order. In the third millennium, machines will play a greater role than physical force. The whole concept of war and armies will change. As physical force as a major factor of change disappears, I see the patriarchal society giving way to a matriarchal one. I see a very different world as we move deeper and deeper into the new millennium, century by century. I am also sure that the most dramatic changes in the quality of life for earth as we progress in time will be just as fantastic and unanticipated, as astronauts and cybernetics would have been to the citizens of 999.

Benazir Bhutto

Ms. BENAZIR BHUTTO   ISLAMABAD, PAKISTAN 1998

Photo by Reuters/Archive Photos

HELMUT SCHMIDT

Birthplace:
Hamburg, Germany

Age at the
Millennium: 82

As the chancellor of Germany from 1974 to 1982, Helmut Schmidt oversaw Germany's rapid emergence as an economic power. Schmidt worked to improve U.S./German partnering (Nixon through Reagan) and European unification via the EEC.

United Nations Nations Unies
NEW YORK   GENÈVE

The new century would be blessed if all of us would more than hitherto stress and live up to the moral principle of any human being's responsibility.

15 A skilled diplomat, Terry Waite negotiated the release of numerous hostages in the Middle East throughout the 1980s. Waite himself was kidnapped in Beirut, held more than four years, and presumed dead by his British home office.

**Birthplace:
Bollington, England**

**Age at the
Millennium: 61**

DR. TERRY WAITE

United Nations   Nations Unies
NEW YORK   GENÈVE

Future generations will be amazed that it took world leaders so long to take the steps needed in order to protect the environment.

Jerry Waite.
1997.

Address

TERRY WAITE

SUFFOLK,

ENGLAND

U.K.

©
UNITED
NATIONS

Future generations will be amazed that it took world leaders so long to take the steps needed in order to protect the environment.

Photo by Gemma Levine

CHRIS PATTEN

Birthplace:
London, England

**Age at the
Millennium: 56**

As Hong Kong's last governor, Chris Patten often angered Beijing during his five-year term with numerous pro-democracy efforts. On July 1, 1997, Patten lowered the British flag for the last time, handing over the Crown Colony to China.

United Nations   Nations Unies
NEW YORK   GENÈVE

I predict that personality and unexpected events will continue to shape history in unpredictable ways, and that technology will help to ensure that liberal values triumph in the next century.

February 1998

Address

©
UNITED
NATIONS

I predict that personality and unexpected events will continue to shape history in unpredictable ways, and that technology will help to ensure that liberal values triumph in the next century.

As president of India for seven years, Ramaswamy Venkataraman served as the head of state of a nation of 900 million people. During his terms, Venkataraman dealt with continuing tensions with Pakistan and the 1991 assassination of Rajiv Gandhi.

Birthplace:
Bombay, India

Age at the Millennium: 79

RAMASWAMY VENKATARAMAN

If the primordial Man has advanced from a mere beast to a civilised being with qualities of kindness, compassion, aesthetic appreciation of literature, art and culture, and living in peace and harmony with fellow men, there is no reason why Man cannot advance further eliminating wars, violence and terrorism, sharing the wealth of the universe equitably among peoples of the world and achieving universal brotherhood. It is my hope that by the end of the year 3000 A.D., the world will be marching towards that goal notwithstanding contra indications at the present.

R Venkataraman.

Address

Mr R. Venkataraman,
Former President of India,

New Delhi
        (India)

HIS HIGHNESS, KING SIHANOUK

Birthplace: Phnom Penh, Cambodia

Age at the Millennium: 78

Becoming king of Cambodia at age 19, Norodom Sihanouk negotiated his country's independence from France and kept Cambodia controversially neutral during most of the neighboring Vietnam War. Later exiled by Pol Pot, Sihanouk returned as king in 1991.

In my humble opinion, the Christian year 2000 doesn't mean the end of the world as predicted by some millennium theorists.

However it could mean a decisive phase toward a New World: without war, unnecessary violence, and where would prevail the values of tolerance, compassion, social justice so valued by us Buddhists, but also of searching for mutual understanding, promotion of the rights of people to do as they please, and the respect for the natural environment and the biosphere.

A world where the new technologies and the scientific discoveries will be put at the exclusive service of mankind, refocused at the center of the universal debate.

The design of the "planetary village" would not end up as the work of the minority, but rather the business of all people and nations, without exception.

United Nations   Nations Unies
NEW YORK   GENÈVE

MESSAGE
de
NORODOM SIHANOUK
ROI DU CAMBODGE
pour
LES CEREMONIES DE
COMMEMORATION
DE l'AN 2 000

- "A mon humble avis, l'An 2 000 chrétien ne consacrera pas "la fin du monde", telle que la "prévoient" les thèses millénaristes.

"L'entrée dans le IIIème Millénaire peut par contre marquer une étape décisive vers un Nouveau Monde, si nous le voulons bien : sans guerres, sans violences inutiles, où prévalent les valeurs de tolérance, de compassion, de justice sociale si chères à nous autres Bouddhistes, mais aussi de recherche d'une compréhension mutuelle, de promotion du driot des peuples à disposer d'eux-mêmes, du respect de l'environnement naturel et de la biosphère.

©
UNITED
NATIONS

United Nations   Nations Unies
NEW YORK   GENÈVE

"Un Monde où les nouvelles technologies et les découvertes scientifiques seront mises au service exclusif de la personne humaine, replacée au centre de l'universal débat.

"L'aménagement du "village planétaire" ne saurait être l'apanage d'une minorité, mais bien l'affaire de tous, personnes et peuples, sans exclusives".

©
UNITED
NATIONS

Address

*Nsihanouk
Roi
du
Cambodge*

Le 14 Juillet 1997

Following the unexpected victory of the Socialists in France's 1981 elections, Laurent Fabius joined the cabinet of Francois Mitterand. After holding several posts, Fabius became France's youngest prime minister in 1984 at the age of 37.

**Birthplace:
Paris, France**

**Age at the
Millennium: 54**

LAURENT FABIUS

United Nations   Nations Unies
NEW YORK   GENÈVE

Le terrain naturel des hommes politiques doit être celui de l'analyse et des trente prochaines années davantage que celui des prophéties et du millénaire, aussi limiterai-je mes souhaits à cet horizon.

Celui-ci doit être universellement marqué par l'enracinement de la démocratie, le renforcement des libertés et la continuation du progrès. Il faut pour cela que la connaissance, la solidarité et la notion de temps choisi soient placées au coeur de nos sociétés. Il est indispensable pour la planète, que soient défendus la paix, l'environnement et la nécessité d'un développement durable et harmonieux. Ces quelques mots d'ordre sont simples. Ils n'en sont pas moins essentiels si nous voulons vraiment que les générations futures connaissent une vie meilleure que la nôtre.

Laurent Fabius

**Laurent FABIUS
Septembre 1997
Paris, France**

UNITED
NATIONS

The politicians' natural field must be the analysis of the next thirty years rather than prophecies on the millennium; therefore I will limit my wishes to this horizon.

This field should be universally marked by the deep-rootedness of democracy, the reinforcement of liberties and the continuation of progress. To reach this goal it is necessary that knowledge, solidarity and time choice be placed at the heart of our communities.

It is essential for our planet that peace, the environment and a lasting and harmonious growth be defended. These few passwords are simple; yet they are essential if we really want it to be that the future generations experience life better than ours.

GIULIO ANDREOTTI

Birthplace:
Rome, Italy

Age at the Millennium: 81

A three-time prime minister of Italy, Giulio Andreotti has proven to be one of Italy's most powerful and popular politicians. In addition to holding numerous cabinet posts, Andreotti led his Christian Democrats to three election victories between 1972 and 1992.

United Nations Nations Unies
NEW YORK   GENÈVE

Saranno distintte pacificamente tutte le armi chimiche e nucleari.
Spero molto prima del 3000.

Giulio Andreotti

25 giugno 1997

Address

©
UNITED
NATIONS

All chemical and nuclear weapons will be peacefully destroyed.
I hope this will happen long before the year 3000.

Photo by Foto Luxardo

Originally a music professor, Vytautas Landsbergis became the father of modern Lithuania. Risking Soviet invasion, he declared Lithuania independent in 1991 and became its first president. Within months all other Soviet republics followed, ending the USSR.

Birthplace:
Kaunas, Lithuania

Age at the
Millennium: 68

VYTAUTAS LANDSBERGIS

United Nations   Nations Unies
NEW YORK   **GENÈVE**

I hope, the Earth will survive.

Address

©
**UNITED
NATIONS**

I hope, the Earth will survive.

ELYAKIM RUBINSTEIN

12

Birthplace:
Tel Aviv, Israel

Age at the Millennium: 53

The attorney general of Israel, Elyakim Rubinstein attended the Camp David Accords and later headed negotiations of the 1994 Israel-Jordan Peace Treaty. A former ambassador to the United States, Rubinstein was appointed attorney general by Prime Minister Netanyahu.

Hope for the Third Millennium

Let me open by mentioning that the *Millennium* is a milestone somewhat alien to Jewish tradition since it emanates from early Christianity with all its historical connotations vis a vis Judaism. However it has become an accepted symbolic milestone and as such is deserving of contemplation and reflection, in the spirit of Psalms (90, 4) "For a thousand years are in thine eyes but as yesterday....".

My main hope for the coming Millennium is that human compassion and an eagerness for peaceful co-existence will parallel technological developments. In the past century and a half mankind has witnessed the most fantastic developments in the fields of science, technology and medicine - advances unprecedented in history. These, however, were utilized to foment horrible behavior, previously unknown in such magnitude to humanity. As we enter the Third Millennium the Holocaust and Hiroshima must serve as a reminder, so that world leaders will have the courage and ability to turn us from the course of destruction to a path, which inspired by spirituality and religion, will direct us in the use of the most modern technology for the benefit of mankind and human values. The law is one means to this end, as a desired "lighthouse for social justice". Honesty, conscience, confidence and optimism are others. Then perhaps mankind, including our own war torn part of the world, will witness Isaiah's prophecy: "And they shall beat their swords into ploughshares and their spears into pruning hooks; nation shall not lift up hand against nation; nor shall they learn war anymore" (Isaiah 2, 4).

Elyakim Rubinstein, Attorney General, The State of Israel

From 1973 to 1976, Zaid al-Rifai held the simultaneous posts of Jordan's prime minister, defense minister, foreign minister, and war adviser to King Hussein. Rifai was made prime minister again in 1985 and is now president of the Senate.

Birthplace: Amman, Jordan

Age at the Millennium: 64

ZAID AL-RIFAI

United Nations **Nations Unies**
NEW YORK GENÈVE

Mankind has made more progress over the last century than it had over the last two thousand years. This progress is a fitting stepping-stone into the next millennium. I believe that during the next one thousand years, mankind will create a world free from disease, poverty and armed conflicts. The world will become one large village; its residents citizens of planet earth. The United Nations might well become a world government — a council of nations and peoples, uniting them in one global world order. Mankind will explore the floor of the oceans, and the outer limitless space. It will settle planets, and continue its march towards ever brighter horizons and to climb to ever-greater heights.

Zaid al-Rifai
ZAID AL-RIFAI
AMMAN - JORDAN. 1997

Address

UNITED NATIONS

Mankind has made more progress over the last century than it had over the last two thousand years. This progress is a fitting stepping-stone into the next millennium. I believe that during the next one thousand years, mankind will create a world free from disease, poverty and armed conflicts. The world will become one large village; its residents citizens of planet earth. The United Nations might well become a world government — a council of nations and peoples, uniting them in one global world order. Mankind will explore the floor of the oceans, and the outer limitless space.

It will settle planets, and continue its march towards ever brighter horizons and to climb to ever-greater heights.

Photo by Camera Press Ltd. / Archive Photos

LEE TENG-HUI

Birthplace: Tamsui, Republic of China

Age at the Millennium: 77

The president of the Republic of China since 1988, Lee Teng-hui has overseen his country's democratization for over a decade. Lee has also presided over a rapidly growing economy and is one of Asia's most influential leaders.

LEE TENG-HUI

**PRESIDENT
OF THE
REPUBLIC OF CHINA**

未來一千年，民主政治與自由經濟將成為新世界之發展主流，科技與文明的進步將為人類帶來更大之福祉，同時，也帶來更複雜的挑戰，須賴全體人類攜手克服。

In the next millennium, democracy and free economy will dominate the trend of development in the world. Progress in science, technology and civilization will bring about greater well-being to mankind, but at the same time, will present more sophisticated challenges that require the concerted efforts of all humanity to overcome.

Teng-hui Lee

China's most famous political dissident, Harry Wu spent nineteen years in Chinese slave labor camps (known as "laogai") before fleeing to the United States. Wu writes and lectures around the world to publicize China's human rights abuses and repression.

Birthplace:
Shanghai, China

Age at the
Millennium: 63

DR. HARRY WU

United Nations　Nations Unies
NEW YORK　GENÈVE

Harry Wu

吴弘达

Jan. 8. 1998

中国将同世界各国一起
更自由，更民主，有一个人
享有尊严及权利。
后隔以国家的观念及
界限将消失。地球将
为人类以及也生物共
享有的一个天堂。

Address

©
UNITED
NATIONS

China will be like other countries in the world, with more freedom, more democracy, where every person enjoys more dignity and rights.
The concept and limitations regarding peoples and countries will disappear, the earth will be a paradise where humans and other life forms will coexist and share together.

HAGE GEINGOB

Birthplace:
Windhoek, Namibia

Age at the
Millennium: 59

The prime minister of Namibia since that country was formed, Hage Geingob led Namibia's long-sought independence from South Africa and its apartheid system. Geingob has governed over one of Africa's most prosperous and peaceful countries.

United Nations   Nations Unies
NEW YORK   GENÈVE

18 - 06 - 97

It is my hope that by the end of third millennium, humankind will have learned Address to resolve its differences and conflicts peacefully. Hopefully therefore there will be more harmony globally in all areas of human endeavour.

Geingob

Prime Minister

UNITED NATIONS

It is my hope that by the end of third millennium, humankind will have learned to resolve its differences and conflicts peacefully. Hopefully therefore there will be more harmony globally in all areas of human endeavour.

A two-term prime minister of Iceland, the American-educated Steingrimur Hermannsson originally planned to be an electrical engineer. Hermannsson ran Iceland's scientific Research Council for twenty-one years before entering politics from 1979 to 1991.

Birthplace:
Reykjavik, Iceland

Age at the
Millennium: 72

STEINGRIMUR HERMANNSSON

United Nations   Nations Unies
NEW YORK   GENÈVE

Hopefully, Man will soon enough come to realize that he will not survive on Earth without a healthy environment and a biological diversity. Hopefully, Man will have the wisdom and courage to discontinue his devastating behaviour. and repair some of the damages that have been made. If not, I fear a catastrophe

Iceland, August 21, 1997

Steingrimur Hermannsson

Address

Millennium Committee of N.Y
Box 20292
Dag Hammerskjøld P.C.C

UNITED NATIONS

Hopefully, Man will soon enough come to realize that he will not survive on Earth without a healthy environment and a biological diversity. Hopefully, Man will have the wisdom and courage to discontinue his devastating behaviour and repair some of the damages that have been made. If not, I fear a catastrophe.

BOUTROS BOUTROS-GHALI

Birthplace:
Cairo, Egypt

**Age at the
Millennium: 70**

The former secretary general of the United Nations, Boutros Boutros-Ghali began his career as a key aide to Anwar Sadat in Egypt. An experienced diplomat, Boutros-Ghali became the sixth person to head the United Nations since its formation, serving from 1992 to 1996.

United Nations　　Nations Unies
NEW YORK　　GENÈVE

The road that the international community must travel during the coming decades is difficult and perilous. Single super power hegemony is a transitory phenomenon, but globalization is an irreversible force on a scale heretofore unseen. It is simply undeniable that global problems demand global solutions and that only the truly global mechanism available is the United Nations system. If this system fails, the international community will be compelled to invent a new organisation capable of serving both the singular and collective interests of its member's states, and of integrating into its system the many new nonstate actors on the global scene

Boutros Boutros-Ghali

10 march 1998

UNITED
NATIONS

The road that the international community must travel during the coming decades is difficult and perilous. Single super power hegemony is a transitory phenomenon, but globalization is an irreversible force on a scale heretofore unseen. It is simply undeniable that global problems demand global solutions and that only the truly global mechanism available is the United Nations system. If this system fails, the international community will be compelled to invent a new organization capable of serving both the singular and collective interests of its member states, and of integrating into its system the many new nonstate actors on the global scene.

The first woman to head a former Warsaw Pact government, Kazimira Prunskiene became the prime minister of Lithuania in 1993 following its self-declared independence from the USSR. A professor, Prunskiene now chairs the Lithuanian Women's Party.

Birthplace:
Vilnius, Lithuania

Age at the Millennium: 57

DR. KAZIMIRA PRUNSKIENE

United Nations   Nations Unies
NEW YORK   GENÈVE

Tūkstantmečio pradžioje dar neišvengsime karų, ekologinių, transporto katastrofų, nusikalstamumo, alkoholizmo ir narkomanijos. Tačiau susinaikinimo ir išsigimimo grėsmė aktyvins ir konsoliduos sveikąsias jėgas:

- Lyčių lygių teisių ir galimybių įgyvendinimas sukurs prielaidas taikai, gerovei bei tobulėjimui;
- Mokslo, technikos, informacijos ir mainų dėka žmoniją mažiau varžys erdvės tarpkontinentiniai ir tarpplanetiniai nuotoliai, kultūrų ir ekonominio išsivystymo skirtumai, ims dominuoti bendros humanistinės vertybės;
- Žmonija per 100-200 metų įveiks badą, išmoks pagydyti vėžį, AIDS, kitas ligas, žmogus geriau pažins ir pozityviai įvaldys savo fizinį, intelektualinį, dvasinį ir energetinį potencialą;
- Agresijos ir smurto prevencija per švietimą, kultūrą ir bendravimą įtvirtins žemėje taiką ir darną.

Kazimira-Danutė PRUNSKIENĖ
Prof.habil.dr.
Lietuvos Respublikos Ministrė pirmininkė (1990-91)
Lietuvos Respublikos Seimo narė
Lietuvos moterų partijos pirmininkė

Krivių 53 a - 13
Vilnius / Lithuania

1997 gruodis

At the turn of the century we will not yet have avoided war, ecological and other catastrophes, crime, alcoholism and drug addiction. However, the threat of self-destruction and deformities will lead to action and consolidation of healthy forces:

- *The implementation of gender equality and equal opportunities will create conditions for peace, well-being and improvement;*
- *Due to science, technology and informational exchange, humankind will be less restricted by distances on earth and in space, and differences in culture and development as well as general human values will begin to dominate;*
- *In 100–200 years humankind will win the battle with starvation, find a cure for cancer, AIDS and other diseases, the individual will be more familiar with and will positively take advantage of his/her physical, intellectual, spiritual and energy potential;*
- *The prevention of aggression and violence through education, culture and dialogue will secure peace and goodwill on earth.*

GERRY ADAMS

Birthplace: Belfast, Northern Ireland

Age at the Millennium: 52

Gerry Adams has been the leader of Sinn Fein, the political wing of the Irish Republican Army, since 1982. Once banned from entering the United States, Adams is now perceived as working for a peaceful resolution of the Northern Ireland crisis.

United Nations   Nations Unies
NEW YORK   GENÈVE

21 July 1997

I hope that there will be peace throughout the world; an end to poverty and inequality, and a more inclusive caring humanity. I do not know if this will happen or indeed if our planet can survive but I think we have a duty to ensure that it does. Le goch Sea inhei

Gerry Adams Belfast Ireland.

© UNITED NATIONS

Address

I hope that there will be peace throughout the world; an end to poverty and inequality, and a more inclusive caring humanity. I do not know if this will happen or indeed if our planet can survive but I think we have a duty to insure that it does. (Le goch Sea inhei)

Photo by Ron Sachs / CNP / Archive Photos

The founding president of the island nation of Seychelles, James Mancham led his nation after independence from Britain in 1976. Located in the Indian Ocean, Mancham's country is renowned for having some of the most undisturbed ecosystems on earth.

Birthplace:
London, England

Age at the
Millennium: 67

SIR JAMES R. MANCHAM

I predict that:

"That isolated beaches,
mountain summits,
lonesome valleys
and great prairies
will replace man-made churches
as gathering places for worship
and Godly communication."

Sir James R. Mancham, KBE

26ᵗʰ February 1998

Glacis-sur-Mer
Mahe
Seychelles

Birthplace:
Athens, Greece

Age at the Millennium: 60

The last monarch of Greece, King Constantine inherited the throne at age 19. During Greece's violent civil war of the 1960s, he was forced out of power in a military coup. King Constantine has lived in exile ever since.

United Nations   **Nations Unies**
NEW YORK   **GENÈVE**

Message for the Third Millennium from His Majesty, King Constantine

I am delighted that the Olympic Games have returned to their Greek origin at the beginning of the new millennium. I also whole heartedly wish peaceful cooperation by all nations, especially in the troubled area of the Balkans and Eastern Mediterranean, the cradle of Democracy. For political freedom and tolerance are the prerequisites for a progressive and democratic world.

Democracy is not an easy form of government, calling for a system of checks and balances and the responsibility of every individual. No democracy is safe without the continuing social and economic progress of the people. So it is vital that the leaders in the next millennium remain fully aware of their political and moral responsibilities towards their people and humanity.

Constantine R

©
UNITED NATIONS

The longest-serving prime minister in Luxembourg's history, Pierre Werner led his nation from 1959 to 1984. Werner also chaired EEC committees on monetary union in the early 1970s, which later led to the euro, Europe's new currency.

Birthplace:
Lille, France

Age at the Millennium: 87

PIERRE WERNER

United Nations   Nations Unies
NEW YORK   GENÈVE

Aug 20th 1997

The forthcoming Millennium should further deepen the insight of the Universe on the side of the infinite great as well as of the infinite small. It might recognize the spiritual background i.e. rediscover God!

Address

Pierre Werner
former Prime Minister
Grand-Duchy of
Luxembourg

©
UNITED
NATIONS

The forthcoming millennium should further deepen the insight of the Universe on the side of the infinite great as well as of the infinite small. It might recognize the spiritual background i.e. rediscover God!

Photo by Pit Schneider

13

ARUN GANDHI

Birthplace:
New Delhi, India

Age at the
Millennium: 66

As the grandson of Mahatma Gandhi, Arun Gandhi founded the Gandhi Institute for Non-Violence. A sought-after speaker, particularly on race relations, Gandhi's institute is based in Memphis partly out of respect to Martin Luther King's legacy.

United Nations   Nations Unies
NEW YORK   GENÈVE

1998

Out of the ashes of materialism will rise the spectre of true morality and meaning of life. There will be greater compassion, concern and commitment towards humans and nature by the year 3000.

ARUN GANDHI

© UNITED NATIONS

Address

Out of the ashes of materialism will rise the spectre of true morality and meaning of life.

There will be greater compassion, concern and commitment towards humans and nature by the year 3000.

A career Panamanian military officer, General Manuel Noriega became president in 1987. His involvement with Colombian drug trafficking prompted an American invasion in 1989, during which he was dramatically apprehended. Noriega now serves a forty-year prison term.

Birthplace:
Panama City, Panama

Age at the Millennium: 61

MANUEL NORIEGA

El hombre encontrará en la oración una fuente de poder; para dirigir y disfrutar de sus días terrenales con salud.
La ciencia médica incluirá la oración en su terapia; para el enriquecimiento del sistema inmunológico y antioxidante.
Llegará el momento que merced a la oración, será posible la conquista de infinidad de objetivos de todo tipo: Desde la prevención de enfermedades hasta la «armonía» y visión del futuro Y la resolución de cualquier Conflicto doméstico.

Address

Gen Manuel Noriega

That man will find in prayer a source of power to direct and enjoy his days—with good health.
That medical science will include prayer in its therapy to enrich the immune and antioxidant system.

That time will come when—thanks to prayer—it will be possible to conquer all the objectives of any kind, from preventing of infirmities to the "harmony" and vision of the future and the solution of all domestic conflicts.

ROBERT HAWKE

Birthplace:
Bordertown, Australia

Age at the
Millennium: 71

A four-term prime minister of Australia, Robert Hawke is one of his nation's longest-serving leaders. Hawke's emotional approach to government made him a widely popular politician and greatly contributed to the success of Australia's Labour Party.

United Nations   Nations Unies
NEW YORK   GENÈVE

Address

I believe that the most important thing that will happen in the new millennium (which, incidentally, starts January 1, 2001) will be the proof of extraterrestrial intelligence.

While this will have many aspects of profound significance, nothing is more important in my estimation than the hope that this event will serve to bind together the peoples of planet earth and serve to emphasize the total futility of human conflict between groups and nations.

As Margaret Thatcher's foreign secretary for seven years, Lord Geoffrey Howe successfully dealt with Argentina's invasion of the Falklands and the Thatcher/Reagan doctrine to contain the USSR in its final years. Howe was later made deputy prime minister.

Birthplace:
Port Talbot, England

Age at the
Millennium: 74

LORD GEOFFREY HOWE

United Nations   Nations Unies
NEW YORK   GENÈVE

The Rt. Hon. The Lord Howe of Aberavon, CH, QC

House of Lords

19 *January* 1998

Prediction for the Third Millennium

"Within the next millennium the present diversity of national coinages and notes will be replaced by a single, worldwide and virtually universal currency or similar but more sophisticated medium of financial exchange"

Geoffrey Howe

©
UNITED
NATIONS

TEDDY KOLLEK

Birthplace:
Vienna, Austria

Age at the
Millennium: 89

One of the founders of Israel, Teddy Kollek established the Jewish Agency for Palestine in 1940. Kollek became a minister when Israel was formed and was elected mayor of Jerusalem in 1965, holding the post until his retirement in 1993.

United Nations   Nations Unies
NEW YORK   GENÈVE

If we live through the next Millennium under the principles of Dag Hammarskjold we'll be all right, particularly in Jerusalem, the most heterogeneous city in the world.

Chapter 5

Music and Art

BRUCE R. HORNSBY

Birthplace:
Williamsburg, Va.

**Age at the
Millennium: 46**

A musician who writes and sings his own lyrics, Bruce Hornsby and his former band, The Range, have received ten Grammy nominations. Hornsby is widely regarded as one of the best bluegrass/jazz musicians in America today.

United Nations   Nations Unies
NEW YORK   GENÈVE

Peace in the Middle East

A Robot Mowing Your Lawn

Political Stability & the End of Famine in Africa

Flying from the U.S. to China for Dinner

The Three-Day Work Week

An African-American U.S. President

Bruce R. Hornsby

August 1997

Williamsburg, VA

Address

Bruce R Hornsby

©
UNITED
NATIONS

Peace in the Middle East

A Robot Mowing Your Lawn

Political Stability and the End of Famine in Africa

Flying from the U.S. to China for Dinner

The Three-Day Work Week

An African-American U.S. President

Photo by William Claxton

One of four Beatles, George Harrison performed lead guitar, sitar, and vocals during the group's legendary ten-year run. Known as "The Quiet Beatle," Harrison developed extensive awareness of Eastern philosophies and has led a reclusive lifestyle.

**Birthplace:
Liverpool, England**

**Age at the
Millennium: 57**

GEORGE HARRISON

United Nations   Nations Unies
NEW YORK   GENÈVE

"You WILL ALL BE DEAD"

is my prediction.... Address

George Harrison ॐ ✝

ENGLAND – OXFORDSHIRE

3RD JANUARY 1998

UNITED NATIONS

"You will all be dead" is my prediction . . .

Photo by Howard Waggner / Fotos International / Archive Photos

PETE SEEGER

Birthplace:
New York, N.Y.

Age at the Millennium: 81

One of America's greatest folk singers, Pete Seeger was one of the first artists to introduce social issues into his music. His songs about civil rights, Vietnam, and the environment earned him a massive following.

United Nations Nations Unies
NEW YORK GENÈVE

May 1, 1997 Beacon, N.Y.

By the year 3000 we (the human species) will have learned to share * or there will be no more humans — and perhaps no life - on earth. Science and technology are giving us all sorts of exciting information, but not the Knowledge or wisdom of how to use it. *Pete Seeger*

* the food, the space, The work, the fun, the joy, - the pain - and the power.

© UNITED NATIONS

By the year 3000 we (the human species) will have learned to share*
or there will be no more humans—and perhaps no life—on earth.
Science and technology are giving us all sorts of exciting information,
but not the knowledge or wisdom of how to use it.

Photo by Andrew de Lory

*the food, the space, the work, the fun, the joy,—the pain—and the power.

43 A consistently successful recording artist, Kenny Loggins's songs include "What a Fool Believes," "Footloose," and "We Are the World." A Grammy winner with ten albums, Kenny—with wife Julia—have also authored a book and promote environmental causes.

Birthplace:
Everett, Wash.

Age at the Millennium: 53

KENNY & JULIA LOGGINS

We believe mankind is now at a crossroads, a "choice-point". I believe we will either destroy ourselves in a series of non-actions resulting in an ecological self-annihilation followed by physical self-destruction in the form of wars, brought on by collective denial and self-hate, or we will experience a mass awakening or both. Quite a few so-called "Indigenous peoples" have predicted a coming "time of the woman". I interpret this to mean a shift in collective consciousness from the "male mind/ego/struggle" approach to life to a "female heart/intuition/cooperative one. If this happens, it will be a gift of grace from a Divine Spirit of Life Itself concerned only with what best serves our physical/spiritual evolution. Julia and I suspect the coming millenium will see a combination of both concepts, such is the nature of the polarity between "good + evil, yes and no, love and hate". One thing is for sure... it will not look like a rerun of the 20th century!

Kenny + Julia Loggins

We believe mankind is now at a crossroads, a "choice-point." I believe we will either destroy ourselves in a series of non-actions resulting in an ecological self-annihilation followed by physical self-destruction in the form of wars, brought on by collective denial and self-hate, or we will experience a mass awakening or both. Quite a few so-called "indigenous peoples" have predicted a coming "time of the woman." I interpret this to mean a shift in collective consciousness from the "male mind/ego/struggle" approach to life to a "female heart/intuition/cooperative" one. If this happens, it will be a gift of grace from a Divine Spirit of Life Itself concerned only with what best serves our physical/spiritual evolution. Julia and I suspect the coming millennium will see a combination of both concepts, such is the nature of the polarity between "good and evil, yes and no, love and hate." One thing is for sure . . . it will not look like a rerun of the 20th century!

PHIL COLLINS

Birthplace:
London, England

Age at the
Millennium: 49

One of the most successful musicians in the history of rock, Phil Collins began his career with the band Genesis in 1971. By 1981 he and Peter Gabriel had left the band. Collins's solo career has included eight major albums and numerous Grammy Awards.

United Nations · Nations Unies
NEW YORK · GENÈVE

We have to learn to understand our fellow man and be considerate of his beliefs & religion. Without this we will self-destruct.

Address

Phil Collins
PHIL COLLINS

©
UNITED
NATIONS

We have to learn to understand our fellow man and be considerate of his beliefs and religion. Without this we will self-destruct.

5 One of America's most popular singers, Andy Williams began as a child star and by 1962 had his own weekly television show. Williams has seventeen gold albums, three Emmys, and six Grammys to his name.

Birthplace:
Wall Lake, Iowa

Age at the Millennium: 70

ANDY WILLIAMS

United Nations   Nations Unies
NEW YORK   GENÈVE

With in the next Millennium:

1. A tenor will be elected president
2. Moon River will be the only non–polluted body of water on EARTH
   AND
3. The ANDY WILLIAMS Christmas show will be transmitted annually to all planets with cable.

Andy Williams

© UNITED NATIONS

Address

Within the next millennium:

1. A tenor will be elected president

2. Moon River will be the only non-polluted body of water on Earth.

AND

3. The Andy Williams Christmas Show will be transmitted annually to all planets with cable.

Photo by Archive Photos

LORD YEHUDI MENUHIN

Birthplace:
New York, N.Y.

Age at the Millennium: 84

One of the greatest performers in classical music, Lord Yehudi Menuhin began playing the violin at age 3. He has toured the world since the 1930s, including entertaining Allied troops during World War II. He was knighted by Queen Elizabeth II in 1965 and later made a lord.

United Nations   Nations Unies
NEW YORK   GENÈVE

handwritten postcard

- *A huge decrease in population—*
- *A new beginning—*
- *A global order in tune with and protecting autonomous, independent cultures—*
- *A new assessment of values—*

- *A great sadness—*
- *Many prayers—*

Photo by Archive Photos

Australia's most famous pianist, David Helfgott gained worldwide fame following the Academy Award–winning film *Shine*, which was based on his life. A child prodigy who once suffered a severe breakdown, Helfgott now tours the world as a concert pianist.

Birthplace:
Melbourne, Australia

Age at the Millennium: 53

DAVID HELFGOTT

United Nations   Nations Unies
NEW YORK   **GENÈVE**

THIRD MILLENNIUM

THINGS POSITIVE – A
TRIUMPH OF THE HUMAN
SPIRIT – IT SURVIVED –
LOVE – JOY – TOLERANCE –
GEMS OF WORDS AND
THOUGHTS NOT GREED OR
ANGER
LOVE

DAVID HELFGOTT
1997

Address

© UNITED NATIONS

David Helfgott

Third Millennium
Things positive—a triumph of the human spirit—it survived—
love—joy—tolerance—gems of words and thoughts not greed or anger
love

DR. OSCAR E. PETERSON

Birthplace:
Montreal, Canada

Age at the
Millennium: 75

One of the all-time great jazz musicians, Oscar Peterson accompanied Louis Armstrong and Duke Ellington before getting his own start in 1949. A revolutionary musician, Peterson also holds a doctorate in musicology.

United Nations   Nations Unies
NEW YORK   GENÈVE

I am hopefully predicting that technology will be employed in our government circles to an extent that will give the ordinary voter and citizen a more acute awareness of every move or intended move to be made by the politicians that they have voted into office. This would therefore give every voting citizen a much clearer view of how their objectives and aims, as exemplified by their vote, are heeded and hopefully attended to by the party members enjoying the confidence of their vote. This would also eradicate the area of any misuse of public funds and taxes.

Address

Dr. Oscar E. Peterson
March, 1997

© UNITED NATIONS

Photo by Al Gilbert, F.R.P.S., Toronto, Canada

49   One of the most popular nightclub performers in Las Vegas, Robert Goulet's early recordings included a 1962 album with Judy Garland. Goulet enjoyed a brief acting career and has since developed a wide following for his often whimsical style.

Birthplace:
Lawrence, Mass.

Age at the Millennium: 67

ROBERT GOULET

United Nations
NEW YORK

Nations Unies
GENÈVE

I can only hope that the people who inhabit this tiny blue orb, oh so tiny and small in our vast universe, will come to their senses and live in harmony and peace.

Else, Hell will be on Earth!

Robert Goulet

Las Vegas, Nevada, U.S.A.   1997

©
UNITED
NATIONS

Photo by Bob Scott / Archive Photos

VLADIMIR ASHKENAZY

Birthplace:
Gorky, Russia

Age at the
Millennium: 63

An accomplished Russian pianist, Vladimir Ashkenazy defected to the West in 1962 after winning an international competition. He took up residence in London and Iceland, later becoming the conductor of the Royal Philharmonic Orchestra.

United Nations   Nations Unies
NEW YORK   GENÈVE

I don't predict.
I only _hope_ that mankind will give more attention to the ethical and spiritual values in life; But knowing human nature I am not too sure of that. As for technological "progress" — it will probably go on: space travel, more knowledge about the origins of life — good luck for that — But people need generosity of the spirit, tolerance and peace.   V. Ashkenazy

Address

from
Vladimir Ashkenazy
March 22 1997.
Switzerland

I don't predict, I only hope *that mankind will give more attention to the ethical and spiritual values in life; but knowing human nature I am not too sure of that. As for technological "progress"—it will probably go on: space travel, more knowledge about the origins of life—good luck for that— But people need generosity of the spirit, tolerance and peace.*

Photo by Decca / Vivianne Purdom

A pioneer of the jazz movement, Sonny Rollins established his own group in 1957. Rollins's hard "bop" style of modern jazz later grew to incorporate calypso, soul, and rock elements.

Birthplace:
New York, N.Y.

Age at the Millennium: 71

SONNY ROLLINS

United Nations   Nations Unies
NEW YORK   GENÈVE

Wouldst that an alien invasion
from outer space unites our
diverse populations. Wouldst
that our greed abates before
we turn this green earth
barren. 21st Century, here
we come!!

Sonny Rollins

Address

Sonny Rollins
Germantown, New York   1997

©
UNITED
NATIONS

Photo by Frank Driggs / Archive Photos

STAN LEE

Birthplace:
New York, N.Y.

**Age at the
Millennium: 78**

One of America's greatest cartoonists, Stan Lee is best known for creating the character Spiderman. His other creations at Marvel Comics include *The Incredible Hulk* and *Fantastic Four*. Lee's work has developed a cult following.

United Nations   Nations Unies
NEW YORK   GENÈVE

In the future, I predict the word "minorities" will become obsolete. As today's world grows ever more fragmented, with so many races and religions, we will come to realize we're *all* part of some minority of one sort or another. For, if the human race is to survive and fulfill its destiny, we must finally accept the fact that diversity is part of humanity's heritage-- and every so-called "minority" has its essential place in the Creator's master plan. Only then might the glorious goal of "Peace on Earth" be realized.

©
UNITED
NATIONS

Address

Stan Lee

LOS ANGELES
CA
U.S.A.

1/26/98

◆   ◆   ◆   ◆   ◆

A newspaper artist after serving in World War II, Bil Keane soon became a full-time cartoonist. His best-known feature, *Family Circus*, began in 1960 and continues as one of America's longest-running and favorite cartoon strips.

Birthplace: Philadelphia, Pa.

Age at the Millennium: 78

United Nations · Nations Unies
NEW YORK · GENÈVE

DURING THE NEXT CENTURY THE BEST HUMOR IN THE HISTORY OF MANKIND (AND WOMANKIND, OF COURSE) WILL BE CREATED. AND THERE WILL STILL BE PEOPLE WHO SAY, "I DON'T GET IT!"

Address

LOVE, BIL KEANE PARADISE VALLEY ARIZONA, 1997

(·) UNITED NATIONS

During the next century the best humor in the history of mankind (and womankind, of course) will be created. And there will still be people who say, "I don't get it!"

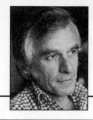

Birthplace:
New York, N.Y.

Age at the Millennium: 71

The artist best known for his forty years with *MAD* magazine, Mort Drucker is one of the most successful freelance cartoonists in America. With a reputation for terrific wit, Drucker's work has included movie posters and covers for *Time* magazine.

United Nations   Nations Unies
NEW YORK   GENÈVE

MY PREDICTION REGARDING THE THIRD MILLENNIUM IS THE DEVELOPMENT OF A SPACE PROGRAM THAT WILL BRING FURTHER KNOWLEDGE OF OTHER PLANETS BEYOND OUR SOLAR SYSTEM.

MY HOPE FOR THE THIRD MILLENNIUM IS THAT WE WILL HAVE PEACE AMONG NATIONS ON THIS MAGNIFICENT PLANET, EARTH.

DRUCKER
WOODBURY, NEW YORK
FEBRUARY, 1998

My prediction regarding the third millennium is the development of a space program that will bring further knowledge of other planets beyond our solar system.

My hope for the third millennium is that we will have peace among nations on this magnificent planet, Earth.

Having created the tremendously popular cartoon strip *Beetle Bailey* in 1950, Mort Walker began a syndicated series that continues today. Walker's humorous portrayal of military life was drawn on many of his own experiences.

Birthplace:
El Dorado, Kans.

Age at the Millennium: 77

MORT WALKER

BY THE YEAR 3,000 I SEE PRES. CLINTON'S HEIRS DENYING ANY INVOLVEMENT IN THE WHITEWATER CASE.

THE NATIONAL DEBT WILL BE A GAZILLION TRILLION + .03

THE YANKEES WILL HAVE WON THEIR 1,032nd PENNANT. (THEY LOST IN THE YEAR 2,547.)

PEOPLE WILL BE LAUGHING AT "I LOVE LUCY" RERUNS.

INTERNAL REVENUE WILL BE INSISTING THAT THEY REALLY, REALLY, REALLY, REALLY JUST WANT TO HELP.

SOMEONE ASKED WHAT A DOLLAR WAS.

THEY EXCAVATED AND FOUND A MALL WITH SIX HUSBANDS STILL WAITING FOR THEIR WIVES.

THE DISNEY COMPANY SELLS THE U.S. TO WAYNE HUIZENGA.

STILL LOOKING FOR THE REAL KILLER IN THE O.J. SIMPSON CASE.

SGT. SNORKEL PREDICTS HE WILL CATCH BEETLE SOON.

MORT WALKER
BOCA RATON, FL 4/28/97

By the year 3,000 I see Pres. Clinton's heirs denying any involvement in the Whitewater Case.

The national debt will be a gazillion trillion + .03.

The Yankees will have won their 1,032nd pennant. (They lost in the year 2,547.)

People will be laughing at "I Love Lucy" reruns.

Internal Revenue will be insisting that they really, really, really, really just want to help.

Someone asked what a dollar was.

They excavated and found a mall with six husbands still waiting for their wives.

The Disney Company sells the U.S. to Wayne Huizenga.

Still looking for the real killer in the O.J. Simpson case.

Sgt. Snorkel predicts he will catch Beetle soon.

DR. KATE MILLETT

Birthplace: Saint Paul, Minn.

Age at the Millennium: 66

Both an artist and writer, Kate Millett established herself as a leader in the feminist movement of the 1970s with her written and visual works. A Ph.D. at Columbia, Millett also founded the Women's Art Colony Farm.

15

United Nations   Nations Unies
NEW YORK   GENÈVE

New York City December 30 1997

Address

The next millennium will see the End of Patriarchy and male Domination. It will also focus on economic justice after a time of greed and global markets. Race and class will be the issues solved.

Kate Millett

© UNITED NATIONS

The next millennium will see the end of patriarchy and male domination. It will also focus on economic justice after a time of greed and 'global markets'. Race and class will be the issues solved.

Photo by James L. Mairs

Perhaps the world's foremost avant-garde artist, Christo, with wife, Jeanne-Claude, has controversially "wrapped" giant objects since the 1960s. Taking years to complete, Christo's projects have included cars, trees, buildings, coastlines, and even islands (Biscayne Bay, 1980–1983).

**Birthplace:
Gabrovo, Bulgaria**

**Age at the
Millennium: 65**

CHRISTO AND JEANNE-CLAUDE

United Nations
NEW YORK

Nations Unies
GENÈVE

A Message for the Third Millennium:

"When men lack a sense of awe, there will be disaster."

Lao-Tzu   (6th Century B.C.)

Written By the Artists:

Christo

Christo

Jeanne-Claude

Jeanne-Claude

**New York, New York
1998**

UNITED
NATIONS

Photo by Transglobe / Archive Photos

LEROY NEIMAN

Birthplace:
Saint Paul, Minn.

Age at the
Millennium: 73

The premier sports artist of the twentieth century, LeRoy Neiman's popular and bright paintings have developed into a virtual industry. Neiman has been sought out to be the "official artist" of everything from Olympic Games to Super Bowls.

United Nations   **Nations Unies**
NEW YORK   GENÈVE

Address

You can always depend on change
Make your contribution to change for the betterment of mankind

LeRoy Neiman
7-17-'97

UNITED NATIONS

You can always depend on change.
Make your contribution to change for the betterment of all mankind.

Photo by Paul Chapnick

159

One of the major American artists of the first half of the twentieth century, Paul Cadmus is known for his controversial art. His paintings usually combine wit and social protest, and are uniquely American.

Birthplace:
New York, N.Y.

Age at the Millennium: 96

PAUL CADMUS

United Nations   Nations Unies
NEW YORK   GENÈVE

In the years 2000 – 3000 I foresee nothing but increasing deterioration in the world. EVERYTHING worsens : overpopulation thrives insanely, international poverty multiplies grotesquely, environmental conditions wither disastrously, privacy is beleaguered, governmental interference in the lives of all is magnified.

Perhaps, if utilized humanely, medical, scientific knowledge may improve the chances of longer life... But will those lives be worth living? I much doubt it.

Address   *Paul Cadmus*

June 23 1997
Weston, CT.   U.S.A.

©
UNITED NATIONS

In the years 2000–3000 I foresee nothing but increasing deterioration in the world. Everything worsens: overpopulation thrives insanely, international poverty multiplies grotesquely, environmental conditions wither disastrously. Privacy is beleaguered, governmental interference in the lives of all is magnified.

Perhaps, if utilized humanely, medical, scientific knowledge may improve the chances of longer life. . . . But will those lives be worth living? I much doubt it.

Photo by Archive Photos

BOB KANE

Birthplace:
New York, N.Y.

**Age at the
Millennium: 84**

The creator of the character Batman, Bob Kane published the first *Batman* comic book in 1939. Kane's character would not only become an American icon over the next six decades, but yield hugely popular television and film adaptations.

United Nations   Nations Unies
NEW YORK   GENÈVE

GIVEN WHAT MANKIND AS A WHOLE HAS ACHIEVED THE LAST THOUSAND YEARS, I PREDICT IN THE NEXT THOUSAND YEARS, WE SHALL EXPERIENCE INTER-PLANETARY TRAVEL AND COLONIZATION ON THE MOON AND OTHER PLANETS. . . . MY HOPE FOR THE FUTURE IS THAT MANKIND SHALL EVOLVE TO A HIGHER SPIRITUAL PLANE WHEREBY WE CAN ACCEPT RESPONSIBILITY FOR OUR ACTIONS -- RELEASE OUR NEED TO DOMINATE, CONTROL, AND EXPLOIT ONE ANOTHER -- AND LEARN TO LIVE IN TRUE HARMONY AND PEACE WHETHER HERE ON EARTH OR ELSEWHERE.

*BOB KANE,
LOS ANGELES,
MARCH, 1998*

©
UNITED
NATIONS

One of the finest photographers in the United States, David Plowden's art is best known for its careful recordings of the American industrial landscape—particularly trains. Plowden has published nineteen books of his work.

Birthplace: Boston, Mass.

Age at the Millennium: 68

DAVID PLOWDEN

I keep remembering that after Pandora closed the box, after all the scourges had been loosed, the only thing that did not escape was hope.

Photo by Sandra S. Plowden, Copyright 1992

Birthplace:
St. Louis, Mo.

Age at the
Millennium: 97

In an art career extending eight decades, Al Hirschfeld joined the *New York Times* in the 1920s. Hirschfeld's caricatures, particularly of Broadway and movie entertainers, have become a legendary part of the art world.

United Nations   Nations Unies
NEW YORK   GENÈVE

APART FROM TECHNOLOGICAL
PROGRESS÷I IMAGINE MORALITY
AND ART WILL REMAIN PRETTY
MUCH THE SAME

HIRSCHFELD

4/20/97 NEW YORK, N.Y.

Address

©
UNITED
NATIONS

Apart from technological progress—I imagine morality and art will remain pretty much the same.

Photo by Susan W. Dryfoos

Chapter 6

Literature

One of the most successful writers ever, James Michener authored novels so epic that he frequently employed research staffs. In his life he gave over $100 million to charity. Mr. Michener passed away in 1997 at age 90.

United Nations   Nations Unies

At age 90 I think a great deal about the oncoming millennium. I see it mainly as the age of the computer, in which this mechanical marvel will speed all aspects of thought and create new aspects about which not even dreamers like me can anticipate. I am fairly confident that animals can continue to be cloned the way they have been in Scotland and that the cloning of humans may not be far behind. As a man with faulty kidneys, which give me a great deal of trouble, I would look forward joyously if the cloning of either animals or human beings meant a reliable supply of new kidneys. Concerning the improvement of the human species so that war or other criminal behavior is no longer possible, I have not much hope. But that the oncoming millennium will be wildly exciting, I have no doubt whatever.

James A. Michener

James A. Michener
Austin, Texas   1997

A great American writer, Gore Vidal's novels have been praised for their portrayals of history and his increasingly sharp satire. Often critical of American society, Vidal has lived in Italy since the 1980s.

Birthplace:
West Point, N.Y.

Age at the
Millennium: 75

GORE VIDAL

Much of the next millennium will be devoted to escape from a planet where, among other inconveniences, thanks to over-population and poisonous agricultural-industrial practises, the water supply has given out. A busy time, desalinating the oceans while sending colonies to rocks not designed for us.

I also suspect the next major religion will feature a voluntary suicide gospel, to thin us out, as it were, joyously.

Address

Gore Vidal

© UNITED NATIONS

SIR ARTHUR C. CLARKE

Birthplace:
Minehead, England

Age at the
Millennium: 83

The greatest science-fiction writer of the century, Sir Arthur C. Clarke also invented the concept of satellite technology. Clarke has sold over one hundred million copies of his fifty-five books, including *Childhood's End* and the *Rama* and *2001* series.

United Nations   Nations Unies
NEW YORK   GENÈVE

SOMETIME
BETWEEN
2000 & 3000 -
PROOF OF
INTELLIGENT
LIFE
ELSEWHERE

Address

ARTHUR C
CLARKE

COLOMBO

SRI LANKA

©
UNITED
NATIONS

Sometime between 2000 and 3000—proof of intelligent life elsewhere.
(additional card: Between 2000 and 2500—major damage by meteor impact.)

Authors' Note: *Readers seeking a truly detailed prediction of the Third Millennium from Dr. Clarke are encouraged to read 3001—The Final Odyssey, published in 1997.*

Photo by Reuters/Anuruddha Lokuhapuarachchi/Archive Photos

With over 400 books to her name, Dame Barbara Cartland is the most successful romance novelist in history. First published in 1923, she has since been knighted by Queen Elizabeth II. Cartland was the step-grandmother of Princess Diana.

Birthplace:
Edgbaston, England

Age at the Millennium: 99

DAME BARBARA CARTLAND

United Nations   Nations Unies
NEW YORK   GENÈVE

     In the Millenium I think we will all travel much faster, but I hope our brains will also become faster!

     I hope that women will stay at home and take care of their children, because at the moment it is the child that suffers if a woman wants a career as well as a child.

     If a woman marries she should concentrate on her husband and children, before considering an additional career.

     DAME BARBARA CARTLAND, D.B.E. D.St.J.
Hertfordshire, England - January 7 1998.

Address

© UNITED NATIONS

FRANK DEFORD

Birthplace:
Baltimore, Md.

Age at the
Millennium: 62

The lead writer of *Sports Illustrated* for twenty-five years, Frank Deford left *SI* in 1989 to pursue freelance and editorial work with the nation's largest magazines and networks. Deford has won an unprecedented six Sportswriter of the Year Awards.

United Nations   Nations Unies
NEW YORK   GENÈVE

September 30, 1997 AD

Race will all but disappear
as an issue in the next one
thousand years. We humans
will move about and inter-
marry, and, in that way diminish
the phsyical differences among
us. Oh yes, in the year 3000
there will still be arguments.
We will, after all, always be
human beings. But we will
argue much more as members of
the same family of humankind
than as different strains in
a species. Anyway:

Let us pray.

Address

from: Frank Deford
      Westport, Connecticu
      United States

©
UNITED
NATIONS

Photo by Reuters / Mike Segar / Archive Photos

A police officer for fifteen years, Joseph Wambaugh drew on his LAPD experiences to write numerous crime novels. Wambaugh's works include *Blue Knight*, *Floaters*, and *The Onion Field*, for which he won an Edgar Allen Poe Mystery Writers Award.

Birthplace:
Pittsburgh, Pa.

Age at the Millennium: 63

JOSEPH WAMBAUGH

United Nations   Nations Unies
NEW YORK   GENÈVE

The printed word shall vanish completely in the coming century, and with it the act of sober reflection. This bodes ominous for the peoples of the next millennium.

Joseph Wambaugh
Author of books
San Diego, California
6 June 1997

©
UNITED NATIONS

The printed word shall vanish completely in the coming century, and with it the act of sober reflection. This bodes ominous for the peoples of the next millennium.

RITA DOVE

Birthplace:
Akron, Ohio

Age at the
Millennium: 47

The first African American woman to be United States poet laureate, Rita Dove received acclaim at age 33 when awarded a Pulitzer Prize for her poem "Thomas and Beulah." Her contemporary poetry is widely praised.

United Nations   Nations Unies
NEW YORK   GENÈVE

> We will either learn to walk with grace along truth's seam, or we will sink into confusion and wallow in our own fear.
> —Rita Dove, 1997

©
UNITED
NATIONS

Address

Rita Dove
English Dept.
University of Virginia
Charlottesville, VA

We will either learn to walk with grace along truth's seam, or we will sink into confusion and wallow in our own fear.

Photo by Fred Viebahn (Charlottesville, Va.)

America's most famous and articulate feminist, Gloria Steinem began as a freelance journalist publicizing women's rights issues. In addition to several books, Steinem founded *Ms.* magazine in 1971, serving as its editor until 1987.

Birthplace:
Toledo, Ohio

Age at the
Millennium: 66

GLORIA STEINEM

United Nations   Nations Unies
NEW YORK   GENÈVE

2000 is a created number, with little meaning for the first cultures on this and other continents, or for many in the modern world who calculate time from different units. This is not the millennium but one more precious day and year on this fragile Space Ship Earth.

Address

2000 is a created number, with little meaning for the first cultures on this and other continents, or for many in the modern world who calculate time from different units. This is not the millennium but one more precious day and year on this fragile Space Ship Earth.

Photo by Frank Capri / Saga / Archive Photos

DR. SHERWIN B. NULAND

Birthplace:
New York, N.Y.

Age at the Millennium: 70

Both a writer and medical doctor, Sherwin Nuland wrote books throughout his thirty-year career as a surgeon at Yale. In 1994, Nuland's controversial *How We Die: Reflections on Life's Final Chapter* made him America's foremost bioethicist.

United Nations   Nations Unies
NEW YORK   GENÈVE

1 Scientists will have the technology to selectively determine the timing and location of all precipitation, but society will elect not to use it or any other controls over weather.

2. There will be a single world government, including a chief executive binding laws and constitution (i.e. a united states of the World). Paradoxically, this will have encouraged increased emphasis on preserving the distinctiveness of ethnic and regional cultures its many states,

3. Cash will not exist. All money transactions will be electronic.

1997

Address

Sherwin B. Nuland

Hamden CT

UNITED NATIONS

Sherwin B. Nuland

---

1. Scientists will have the technology to selectively determine the timing and location of all precipitation, but society will elect not to use it or any other controls over weather.

2. There will be a single world government, including a chief executive, binding laws and constitution (i.e. a United States of the World). Paradoxically, this will have encouraged increased emphasis

on preserving the distinctiveness of ethnic and regional cultures of its many states.

3. Cash will not exist. All money transactions will be electronic.

Photo by David Ottenstein

A medical graduate of Columbia and Harvard, Robin Cook has applied his medical experiences to a number of suspense novels. Among Cook's best-selling novels are *Outbreak*, *Contagion*, and *Acceptable Risk*.

Birthplace:
New York, N.Y.

Age at the Millennium: 60

DR. ROBIN COOK

A believe that some time soon in the next millennium there will occur a dramatic break through in genetics akin to the elucidation of the structure of DNA. This break through will enable medicine to obviate organ transplants and cause the people of that time to look back on our transplant surgery the way we look back at surgery done without regard to fluid and electrolyte balance. It will be a great step for medicine and mankind and will offer new possibilities for enhancing the quality of life.

Robin Cook M.D.
Naples, Florida
USA
July 20, 1997

I believe that some time soon in the next millennium there will occur a dramatic breakthrough in genetics akin to the elucidation of the structure of DNA. This breakthrough will enable medicine to obviate organ transplants and cause the people of that time to look back on our transplant surgery the way we look back at surgery done without regard to fluid and electrolyte balance. It will be a great step for medicine and mankind and will offer new possibilities for enhancing the quality of life.

Photo by Frank Capri / Saga / Archive Photos

SIDNEY SHELDON

Birthplace:
Chicago, Ill.

Age at the Millennium: 83

A popular novelist, Sidney Sheldon began his career as a producer of several network television shows. In 1970 Sheldon published his first book, soon becoming a prolific writer of suspense thrillers such as *The Other Side of Midnight*.

United Nations   Nations Unies
NEW YORK   GENÈVE

The next millennium will bring miraculous advances in science. Man will be able to harness nature and tame the environment. But the most important task we have before us is to learn to tame man.

Sidney Sheldon

Address

Los Angeles, California
August, 1997

©
UNITED
NATIONS

A former White House reporter and now a managing editor of *Newsweek* magazine, Eleanor Clift is regarded as an elite member of Washington's press corps. Clift's permanent seat on NBC's *The McLaughlin Group* has made her a household name.

Birthplace:
New York, N.Y.

Age at the Millennium: 60

ELEANOR CLIFT

United Nations Nations Unies
NEW YORK GENÈVE

A woman will be elected President, shattering the last glass ceiling. Her husband will hold a press conference to announce he is keeping his DAY jOB. And "CROSSFIRE" will host a debate on whether the office of the First LADy should be made gender neutral. office of the First Person?

Eleanor Clift
WASh. D.C. 1997

A woman will be elected President, shattering the last glass ceiling. Her husband will hold a press conference to announce he is keeping his day job. And "Crossfire" will host a debate on whether the office of the First Lady should be made gender neutral. Office of the First Person?

JOHN JAKES

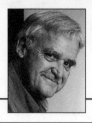

Birthplace:
Chicago, Ill.

Age at the
Millennium: 68

A prolific writer of American historic fiction, John Jakes became famous during the bicentennial era with his eight-volume *Kent Family Chronicles.* Jakes later wrote *North and South* and other epics that were made into television miniseries.

United Nations   Nations Unies
NEW YORK   GENÈVE

By the end of the next century, I envision a multi-cultural United States glowingly different from the nation we inhabit today. The old European culture will still undergird it, but it will be a new land, brightened and enriched by the strengths of peoples from Asia, Africa, Latin America. They will have dropped the hyphens from descriptions of them-selves, as my German-American ancestors did. They will simply be Americans - one of them, perhaps, our lady President (of Asian heritage), with a handsome brown or ebony gentleman her VP (or it could be the other way around). I believe it will be a country with all of our enduring virtues and values but - I pray - fewer hatreds. I have but one regret about this future. I will not see it.

JOHN JAKES

Hilton Head Island SC 1997

UNITED
NATIONS

Photo by Joseph Mick

The author of two renowned detective series, Anne Perry is one of the most popular mystery writers in the world. Using the setting of Victorian-era London, Perry's twenty novels have been translated into several languages.

**Birthplace:
London, England**

**Age at the
Millennium: 62**

ANNE PERRY

United Nations   Nations Unies
NEW YORK   GENÈVE

ANNE PERRY, PORTMAHOMACK, SCOTLAND — UK. 1997.

Even though we will have more scientific advancement, we do not need it in order to reach the full stature of our possibilities.

Now we must look far more deeply within ourselves, take a mirror to our souls ... and deide what we are going to do about that which we see there

I believe the events of the next millennium will force us to do this. There will no longer be spiritual 'middle ground.'

Anne Perry

Even though we will have more scientific advancement, we do not need it in order to reach the full stature of our possibilities.

Now we must look far more deeply within ourselves, take a mirror to our souls . . . and decide what we are going to do about that which we see there.

I believe the events of the next millennium will force *us to do this. There will no longer be spiritual 'middle ground.'*

Photo by Sheila Burnett

HOWARD FAST

Birthplace:
New York, N.Y.

**Age at the
Millennium: 86**

A controversial writer, Howard Fast was blacklisted in the 1940s and 1950s for supporting American communism. During this blacklist period, he wrote *Spartacus*. However, Fast's later work, *The Naked God*, rejected Soviet practices and rejuvenated his career.

17

United Nations   Nations Unies
NEW YORK   GENÈVE

The largest hope I have for the 21st Century is
that finally, at a long last, the nations of
mankind will give up their practice of mutual
murder and destruction, which they call <u>war</u>.

My second hope is that they will do away with
poverty, hunger and disease---and recognize that
the planet earth is their mother and must not
be destroyed.

My third hope---and perhaps my greatest illusion
is that this next 100 years will usher in at least
the beginning of the brotherhood and sisterhood
of humankind.

Howard Fast
Old Greenwich, Conn.
U.S.A.
June 21, 1997

©
UNITED
NATIONS

79   A psychologist specializing in sexual relationships, John Gray is best known for writing *Men
Are from Mars, Women Are from Venus*, which has sold
over six million copies. In addition to writing,
Gray conducts seminars and broadcasts.

Birthplace:
Houston, Texas

Age at the
Millennium: 49

DR. JOHN GRAY

JOHN GRAY, AUTHOR: men Are from Mars,
Women Are from Venus

United Nations   Nations Unies
NEW YORK   GENÈVE

With an increasing understanding of the
differences between men and women,
the quality of relationships and
communication between the sexes will
dramatically improve; divorce will be less.
New non-violent parenting approaches
will create loving and strong families
providing a practical basis for real peace
in the world. John Gray Mill Valley
California
USA

Address

©
UNITED
NATIONS

*With an increasing understanding of the differences between men and
women, the quality of relationships and communication between the sexes
will dramatically improve; divorce will be less. New non-violent
parenting approaches will create loving and strong families providing a
practical basis for real peace in the world.*

Photo by Frank Capri / Saga / Archive Photos

CLIVE CUSSLER

Birthplace: Aurora, Ill.

Age at the Millennium: 69

Perhaps the best writer of undersea adventures, Clive Cussler has authored numerous best-selling suspense novels including *Raise the Titanic*, *Deep Six*, and *Sea Hunters*. Cussler himself has discovered several historic shipwrecks.

United Nations   Nations Unies
NEW YORK   GENÈVE

Nanotechnology... the ability to control the arrangement of atoms and build virtually anything possible under natural law, will become the major breakthrough in science and technology by the year 2060.

Clive Cussler

Telluride, Colorado July 23, 1997

Address

molecular repairs inside human bodies will be possible, manufacturing will be revolutionized, nothing will be impossible to produce cheaply and with quality. Nanotechnology is the way of the future.

©
UNITED
NATIONS

Nanotechnology . . . the ability to control the arrangement of atoms and build virtually anything possible under natural law, will become the major breakthrough in science and technology by the year 2060.

Molecular repairs inside human bodies will be possible. Manufacturing will be revolutionized. Nothing will be impossible to produce cheaply and with quality.

Nanotechnology is the way of the future.

Photo by Paul Peregrine

One of the best espionage writers in the world, Frederick Forsyth's most famous works include *Day of the Jackal, Odessa File,* and *The Dogs of War,* all of which were made into successful motion pictures.

**Birthplace:
Ashford, England**

**Age at the
Millennium: 62**

FREDERICK FORSYTH

United Nations   Nations Unies
NEW YORK   GENÈVE

```
Shortly after the inception of the new Millennium,
the Federal Republic of Europe, essentially a German-
driven engine aimed at Continental domination, will
come into being.
Before the end of the first decade, it will have
collapsed, bringing great economic misery and hardship
to those who chose to participate in it.
```

Frederick Forsyth

©
UNITED
NATIONS

TONY HILLERMAN

Birthplace:
Sacred Heart, Okla.

Age at the
Millennium: 75

A highly popular mystery writer, Tony Hillerman spent most of his career as a journalist in the American West. Drawing from his experiences, Hillerman's books provide characters and situations involving Native American culture.

United Nations   Nations Unies
NEW YORK   GENÈVE

Through the next 1000 years we will see a melding of races into a single homogenized humanity. However, I wonder if the species will endure until 3000 AD. There are many devastating possibilities & our creator may decide to end the experiment

Tony Hillerman

Address
Tony Hillerman
Albuquerque, N.M

©
UNITED NATIONS

Through the next 1000 years we will see a melding of races into a single homogenized humanity. However, I wonder if the species will endure until 3000 AD. There are many devastating possibilities and our creator may decide to end the experiment.

Photo by Barney Hillerman

A prolific writer, George Plimpton formed his own publication, *The Paris Review*, in 1953. He has since written numerous books, on topics ranging from wine to sports to the Kennedys.

Birthplace:
New York, N.Y.

Age at the Millennium: 73

GEORGE PLIMPTON

John Glenn will go into space yet again, sometimes in his mid-eighties, not so much for research as that he truly likes it up there.

George Plimpton

© UNITED NATIONS

John Glenn will go into space yet again, sometime in his mideighties, not so much for research as that he truly likes it up there.

Photo by Frank Capri / Saga / Archive Photos

THOMAS KENEALLY

Birthplace:
Sydney, Australia

**Age at the
Millennium: 65**

Prominent in Australian literary circles since 1967, Thomas Keneally earned an international reputation in 1982 with his novel *Schindler's Ark*. Ten years later Steven Spielberg would adapt the novel into the Oscar-winning motion picture *Schindler's List*.

United Nations   Nations Unies
NEW YORK   GENÈVE

One hopes that in the millennium the huge nation of refugees will find a home.

Tom Keneally

© UNITED NATIONS

One hopes that in the millennium the huge nation of refugees will find a home.

Photo by Kerry Klayman

Herman Wouk's novels, which include *The Caine Mutiny*, *The Holocaust*, and *The Winds of War*, are renowned for their epic detail. Many of his works have been made into Emmy Award–winning television miniseries.

Birthplace:
New York, N.Y.

Age at the Millennium: 85

HERMAN WOUK

War will come to be as obsolete a barbarism of ancient days as human sacrifice.

Herman Wouk

4 May 97
Palm Springs

War will come to be as obsolete a barbarism of ancient days as human sacrifice.

Photo by Yousuf Karsh

GAY TALESE

Birthplace:
Ocean City, N.J.

Age at the Millennium: 68

Described by Tom Wolfe as "the inventor of the new journalism," Gay Talese evolved from a non-fiction journalist at *Esquire* magazine to one of America's most acclaimed novelists. His most famous work is *Honor Thy Father*.

United Nations   Nations Unies
NEW YORK   GENÈVE

June 1, 1997--New York City

I believe that interracial marriage will increase in the next century, increase to a level that racial conflict in the United States will be less pronounced that it has been in the ~~period between 1960 and 1990, thirty years after the Civil Rights movement made its marks.~~ Without interracial marriage there can be no real integration in America; it is the only way that Afro-Americans can be integrated into the main-stream...and I think that this will be a trend, a welcome trend....or else, equality will be impossible in America.

20ℍ Century

Address

Mr Gay Talese

New York, NY

©
UNITED
NATIONS

PETER STRAUB

A prolific novelist of fantasy and horror, Peter Straub has written since the 1970s. He cowrote *The Talisman* with Stephen King, a novelist to whom he is often compared. Many of Straub's novels have been made into motion pictures.

Birthplace: Milwaukee, Wis.

Age at the Millennium: 57

In the absence of a crystal ball, I can still predict: regional wars which expand into wider wars; devastating new viruses and diseases; environmental disasters; bloody racial and religious conflicts, and many other poisonous inheritances from the present century. Yet I cannot but believe that a humane, liberal spirit and mankind's irrepressible inventiveness will not prevail and endure.

PETER STRAUB, New York NY 1/3/98

Address

In the absence of a crystal ball, I can still predict: regional wars which expand into wider wars; devastating new viruses and diseases; environmental disasters; bloody racial and religious conflicts, and many other poisonous inheritances from the present century. Yet I cannot but believe that a humane, liberal spirit and mankind's irrepressible inventiveness will not prevail and endure.

Photo by Frank Capri / Saga / Archive Photos

JACKIE COLLINS

Birthplace:
London, England

Age at the
Millennium: 58

One of the best-known writers of the Hollywood scene, Jackie Collins has written over twenty novels since the 1970s. Her stories of sex, wealth, and fame have been made into screenplays, including several starring her sister, Joan Collins.

United Nations   Nations Unies
NEW YORK   GENÈVE

Address

©
UNITED
NATIONS

A whole new world lies ahead! There will be supermarkets for spare body parts—people will live for two or three hundred years and still be active. Sex will be a thing of the past. Babies will be created in a lab. Hey—I'm glad I'm here now!!

Photo by Greg Gorman

One of America's most acclaimed playwrights, Edward Albee has won numerous Pulitzer Prizes for his work. An institution on Broadway, Albee is best known for *Who's Afraid of Virginia Woolf?*, *The Zoo Story*, and *Seascape*.

**Birthplace:
Washington, D.C.**

**Age at the
Millennium: 72**

EDWARD ALBEE

United Nations   Nations Unies
NEW YORK   GENÈVE

Maybe we can do better next time!

Address

*Edward Albee
New York City*

©
UNITED
NATIONS

Maybe we can do better next time!

Photo by Alan Jeffry

HELEN GURLEY BROWN

Birthplace:
Green Forest, Ark.

Age at the Millennium: 78

Editor of the most consistently popular women's magazine in America, Helen Gurley Brown has headed *Cosmopolitan* magazine since 1965. A prolific feminist writer, Brown's initial fame came from her 1962 book *Sex and the Single Girl*.

190

United Nations   Nations Unies

My Thoughts about the new millennium are simple. I will be grateful to get there and I predict, on advice of my internist, that I shall. As for what will take place during this third millennium, I hope and believe we will have found a cure for cancer; problems with relationships will not get any better, I fear; traffic will be worse; population will increase the discomfort of living on a small planet; an asteroid on a collision course will bring the nations together and reduce the risk of war among ourselves; most predictions will have been proven wrong.

Helen Gurley Brown

Dec.18.1996

Chapter 7

Business and Law

ROBERT MONDAVI

Birthplace:
Virginia, Minn.

Age at the Millennium: 87

The most respected vintner in America, Robert Mondavi spent years refining his skills in vineyards of the Napa and Simi Valleys. In 1966 he formed his own winery, creating standards that have been the model for U.S. wine for the past thirty years.

United Nations — Nations Unies
NEW YORK — GENÈVE

In the next millennium we hope to see the problem of hunger erased, as technology increases the food supply and population is better controlled. But beyond the simple satisfaction of hunger, we will see an increase in interest among all people in the varieties of wines and foods available on the earth. The interest in cuisines will grow, and the wines that accompany them will be more balanced, more elegant and more gentle.

And a Center for Wine, Food and the Arts will be created to celebrate the foods, wines and cultures from all over the world - - I can make that prediction because I am committed to its construction right here in Napa Valley.

Robert Mondavi
June 6, 1997

Napa Valley Calif.

©
UNITED
NATIONS

Prior to cofounding TRW (The Ramo Wooldridge) Co., Simon Ramo was chief scientist of the Pentagon's ICBM program, overseeing the Atlas, Titan, and Minuteman missiles. He also invented microwave technology while at General Electric.

Birthplace:
Salt Lake City, Utah

Age at the
Millennium: 87

DR. SIMON RAMO

January 8, 1998

The **21st Century** will be dominated by science and technology advances, the most influential being in the field of Genetic Engineering.

First will come the suppressing of disease, the slowing of aging, and the production of superior nourishment.

Later the century will see the improvement of the population by gene selection in the process of the creation of life and gene and cellular transplantations in all living beings and matter.

Simon Ramo

Dr. Simon Ramo
Co-founder, TRW Inc.
Beverly Hills, California

ROBERT L. CRANDALL

Birthplace:
Westerly, R.I.

Age at the Millennium: 65

Chairman of the world's largest airline from 1985 to 1998, Robert Crandall made his mark at American Airlines by devising the first frequent flyer program. His tenure as chairman was marked by continued deregulation and impressive expansion.

194

United Nations   Nations Unies
NEW YORK   GENÈVE

At American Airlines, it is our greatest hope that <u>early</u> in the millennium, humankind will effectively use continuing advances in information technology, communications, and transportation to bind itself closer together. We hope for a world in which diversity is better respected, and where people of many cultures can live together in harmony. And we hope our fleet of Silver Birds will help advance that cause.

Robert L. Crandall
Chairman and CEO
American Airlines

Address

The chairman and CEO of the Chrysler Corporation, Robert Eaton has presided over America's fastest growing auto company. Formerly the head of General Motors Europe, Eaton succeeded Lee Iacocca in 1992.

Birthplace:
Buena Vista, Colo.

Age at the Millennium: 60

ROBERT EATON

United Nations   Nations Unies
NEW YORK   GENÈVE

Private transportation will be the primary mode of personal transportation, however, the internal combustion engine will be long gone.

1-28-98

Address

MILLENNIUM COMMITTEE
OF NEW YORK, LLC
45 Rockefeller Plaza
20th Floor
New York, NY 10111

©
UNITED
NATIONS

EDMUND LEOPOLD DE ROTHSCHILD

Birthplace:
London, England

Age at the Millennium: 84

A prominent British banker, Edmund de Rothschild took over the chairmanship of the family exporting business, N. M. Rothschild & Sons, upon the death of his father. He retired in 1994 at the age of 78.

United Nations   Nations Unies
NEW YORK   GENÈVE

SEVERE EARTHQUAKE WEST USA, JAPAN
CLIMATIC CHANGES MANY PARTS OF THE WORLD

CHINA BECOMES DOMINANT POWER IN ASIA

RELIGIOUS PROBLEMS ACUTE, MINOR WARS.

WATER PROBLEMS ACCENTUATED AND PARTIALLY SOLVED

DEMOCRACY UNDER SEVERE DILUTION

COMPUTER ERA, TOSS UP IF BENEFICIAL

SEVERE OVERPOPULATION PROBLEMS AND UNEMPLOYMENT PROBLEMS WILL AFFECT MANY COUNTRIES

POLLUTION PROBLEM WILL BE MOST IMPORTANT FACTOR 21st CENTURY

Address

Edmund Leopold de Rothschild

EXBURY

SOUTHAMPTON

UK

© UNITED NATIONS

Edmund L. de Rothschild   May 1997

Severe earthquake west USA, Japan

Climatic changes many parts of the world

China becomes dominant power in Asia

Religious problems acute, minor wars

Water problems accentuated and partially solved

Democracy under severe dilution

Computer era, toss up if beneficial

Severe overpopulation problems and unemployment problems will affect many countries

Pollution problem will be most important factor 21st century

(additional card: Drug problems accentuated)

Nearly all wheeled transport will be converted to electric means avoidance of CO, and attempts to avoid CO_2 [carbon dioxide])

As chairman of the Gallup Institute, George Gallup heads the nation's largest polling organization. The Gallup Institute was formed in 1936 by Gallup's father, who established the concept of polling as a reliable science.

Birthplace:
Princeton, N.J.

Age at the Millennium: 70

GEORGE GALLUP JR.

United Nations   Nations Unies
NEW YORK   GENÈVE

If the focus of the 20th century has been on outer space, the focus of the 21st century may well be on inner space. Many believe we are entering a new era of discovery -- not of the world around us, but the world within. What had begun so hopefully at the beginning of the century, with the monumental contri-

butions of Wiliam James and others, is now at last being earnestly pursued on the eve of a new century.

The disappointments of the external world; the headlong pursuit of hedonism and materialism; and the callous disregard of people for each other -- all have driven people to look within themselves and to God for ways to understand and deal with life.

George Gallup, Jr.

George Gallup, Jr.

Address

The George H. Gallup
    International Institute

© UNITED NATIONS

DWAYNE O. ANDREAS

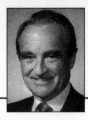

Birthplace:
Worthington, Minn.

Age at the
Millennium: 82

Dwayne Andreas has been the chairman of ADM (Archer Daniels Midland) since 1970. During his tenure he has had astonishing success growing ADM into America's largest agricultural and commodities firm.

United Nations   Nations Unies
NEW YORK   GENÈVE

Western hemisphere free trade,
heretofore an ideological concept,
will become a reality and will
vastly improve the standard of
living throughout the hemisphere.

1997
Archer Daniels Midland Company
Decatur, Illinois

Address

   Dwayne O. Andreas
Chairman of the Board

©
UNITED
NATIONS

Photo by Bachrach

Rumored to be India's wealthiest man, Ratan Tata is chairman of the vast conglomerate Tata Sons Enterprises. Tata oversees a business empire that his family founded in the early 1900s. It is now the largest industrial firm in India.

**Birthplace:
Bombay, India**

**Age at the
Millennium: 63**

RATAN TATA

United Nations   Nations Unies
NEW YORK   **GENÈVE**

Predictions for the Next Millennium:

– There will be a bridge over the Bering Strait, linking North America to Asia.

– Airlines will fly at 3-5 times the speed of sound.

– Cars will be powered with disposable, safe nuclear fuel in a tiny, safe power reactor.

– Genetic engineering will extend life expectancy by 50%.

©
UNITED
NATIONS

Address

RATAN TATA

Chairman of
Tata Industries Ltd.

Signed in Bombay, India
1998

FRED GOLDMAN

Birthplace:
Saint Louis, Mo.

Age at the Millennium: 60

Formerly a successful salesman in Agoura, California, Fred Goldman rose to prominence following his son's 1994 murder and subsequent judgment against O.J. Simpson. After years of court appearances, Goldman coauthored *His Name Is Ron* and founded a victims' rights organization.

My hope for the future is that our legislators and our justice system will act everyday - keeping in mind that their first responsibility is the safety of the citizens. That every time they fail to harshly punish a violent criminal, they put into motion the very conditions that insure another violent crime. That we will no longer tolerate crime or criminals. That the rights of the vast majority of our nation that obey the law everyday will not be held ransom by the system for the minority that commit 100% of the crime. That our legislatures and our justice system will recreate a country in which you and I, our families and our children can feel safe and unafraid. In honor of our victims, there must be change.
ANYTHING LESS IS UNACCEPTABLE!

Fred Goldman - **Ron's Dad**

Agoura, California 91301
January 1998

201

As chairman and CEO of the Fuji Photo Film Co., Minoru Ohnishi runs the world's second largest photographics firm. Highly successful over a fifty-year career, Ohnishi received the Order of the Rising Sun in 1995 from Japan's emperor.

Birthplace: Hyogo Prefecture, Japan

Age at the Millennium: 75

MINORU OHNISHI

United Nations   Nations Unies
NEW YORK   GENÈVE

世界の人々が次の一千年、その
ヒューマンライフの持続的成長
発展に向けて、智慧と能力を発
揮し続けることを確信する。

大切なことは、
(1) グローバルな視点と
　　ローカル文化との調和。
(2) 科学・技術・生産の進歩と
　　地球環境保全との調和。
である。　　　　　1998年3月2日

Address

富士写真フイルム株式会社

取締役会長

大西 實

©
UNITED
NATIONS

I believe that the people of the world will continue to exercise the full scope of their wisdom and ability in the aim of sustainable development throughout the next millennium.
The critical issues will be:

1) harmonization of global perspectives and local cultures, and
2) harmonization of the progress of science, technology and manufacturing with the goal of preserving the Earth's environment.

ESTHER DYSON

Birthplace:
Zurich, Switzerland

Age at the
Millennium: 49

The most influential woman of the computer revolution, Esther Dyson has enjoyed a cult following since the 1970s with her publications on the digital age. A securities analyst, Dyson's earliest recommendations included a start-up firm known as Microsoft.

United Nations   Nations Unies
NEW YORK   GENÈVE

Address

In 2087 and in 2987, I hope we will still be making new mistakes — and learning from them.

(signature)

New York City, 5 January 1998

UNITED NATIONS

Esther Dyson

In 2087 and 2987, I hope we will still be making new mistakes—and learning from them!   Photo by Katherine McGlynn

203 Mentored as a teenager in the restaurant business, Thomas made his mark by purchasing four franchises from Col. Harland Sanders. In 1969 he formed his own restaurant, growing it into the multibillion-dollar Wendy's fast-food chain. Thomas also extensively promotes adoption awareness.

Birthplace:
Atlantic City, N.J.

Age at the Millennium: 68

R. DAVID THOMAS

United Nations   Nations Unies
NEW YORK   GENÈVE

I believe that every child deserves a permanent home and loving family. It is my greatest hope that in the 21st century, children will no longer languish in foster care and every child will be able to grow up with loving and nurturing parents.

Address

Dave Thomas
Founder, Wendy's International

©
UNITED
NATIONS

WILLIAM R. HEWLETT

Birthplace:
Ann Arbor, Mich.

**Age at the
Millennium: 87**

The "Father of Silicon Valley," William Hewlett began an electronics business in his Palo Alto garage in 1938 that is now a landmark. Cofounding Hewlett-Packard, Hewlett's work led to the creation of the first computer processor and the first personal computer.

United Nations   Nations Unies
NEW YORK   GENÈVE

The future will bring new
opportunities for more people
to be exposed to computers
and to use them in a positive
and productive way.

    William R. Hewlett

    Year: 2002
    Location: Everywhere!

Address

©
UNITED
NATIONS

A pioneer of America's weight-loss industry, Jenny Craig has been in the diet and fitness movement since 1959. In 1983, Craig incorporated her business with over 600 weight-loss centers, and has given tens of millions of dollars to charity.

Birthplace:
Berwick, La.

Age at the Millennium: 68

JENNY CRAIG

United Nations Nations Unies
NEW YORK GENÈVE

In the next millennium I see researchers finding a way to control fat storage on our body—resulting in reduced risk of life-threatening obesity related diseases. I see scientist using a form of cloning to replace diseased parts of the human body—thus lengthening our life span. My hope is that we all learn to accept each other's differences so that we may enjoy those extra years on earth in peace and harmony worldwide—

6-7-97

Jenny Craig
Del Mar, California

In the next millennium I see researchers finding a way to control fat storage on our body—resulting in reduced risk of life-threatening obesity related diseases. I see scientists using a form of cloning to replace diseased parts of the human body—thus lengthening our life span. My hope is that we all learn to accept each other's differences so that we may enjoy those extra years on earth in peace and harmony worldwide—

HUGH HEFNER

Birthplace:
Chicago, Ill.

Age at the Millennium: 74

Having published the first mainstream centerfold magazine ever in 1953, Hugh Hefner would become known as the "Father of the Sexual Revolution." By the 1970s, Hefner had built Playboy Enterprises into a multimillion-dollar enterprise.

United Nations   Nations Unies
NEW YORK   GENÈVE

A PREDICTION FOR THE NEW MILLENNIUM—
It will become a cybernetic world in which the walls that seperate us — national, religious and racial — will increasingly disappear in the pursuit of personal, political and economic freedom.

Hugh Hefner

LOS. ANGELES, CA. 1997

UNITED NATIONS

PLAYBOY

A PREDICTION FOR THE NEW MILLENNIUM—
It will become a cybernetic world in which the walls that separate us—
national, religious and racial—will increasingly disappear in the
pursuit of personal, political and economic freedom.

A prosecutor in the "Trial of the Century," Christopher Darden pursued the conviction of O. J. Simpson for over a year. At the conclusion of the case, Darden resigned after fifteen years in the Los Angeles district attorney's office.

Birthplace:
Richmond, Va.

Age at the Millennium: 44

CHRISTOPHER A. DARDEN

United Nations   Nations Unies
NEW YORK   **GENÈVE**

I predict that in the USA— the nation will elect a hispanic as President before electing an African American

Address

Christopher A. Darden
Feb. 2, 1998
Los Angeles, CA

©
UNITED
NATIONS

I predict that in the USA—the nation will elect a hispanic as President before electing an African American.

Photo by Reuters/Sam Mircovich/Archive Photos

ROBERT L. SHAPIRO

Birthplace:
Plainfield, N.J.

**Age at the
Millennium: 58**

One of Hollywood's most prominent defense attorneys and trial lawyers even before the O. J. Simpson trial, Robert Shapiro gained national fame for his assembly and strategy of the "Trial of the Century's" so-called Dream Team.

United Nations   Nations Unies
NEW YORK   GENÈVE

In the next millennium we will have space energy stations transmitting solar energy, thereby freeing the world from pollution.

Robert L. Shapiro
Los Angeles, California
1997

Address

ⓒ
UNITED
NATIONS

Chapter 8

Science and Exploration

DR. EDWARD TELLER

Birthplace:
Budapest, Hungary

Age at the
Millennium: 92

The creator of the hydrogen bomb, Edward Teller is one of the greatest physicists in history. At Los Alamos, Teller worked with Einstein, Fermi, and Oppenheimer, later publicly feuding with Oppenheimer about the morality of defensive nuclear weapons.

United Nations   Nations Unies
NEW YORK   GENÈVE

I EXPECT THAT SOMETIME IN THE
NEXT 1000 YEARS TO FIND
EVIDENCE OF COMMUNICATION
BETWEEN DIFFERENT PLANETS
IN GLOBULAR CLUSTERS WHERE
STARS ARE CLOSER TOGETHER.
THIS COULD LEAD TO GREAT
ADVANCES IN UNDERSTANDING
LIFE AND INTELLIGENCE.

SEPTEMBER 25, 1997

Address

©
UNITED
NATIONS

An anthropologist from Norway, Thor Heyerdahl's 1947 voyage across the Pacific in the hand-built raft *Kon Tiki* sought to prove the origin of Polynesian people. Heyerdahl later investigated numerous other cultures, including the mysterious Easter Island.

Birthplace:
Larvik, Norway

Age at the
Millennium: 86

THOR HEYERDAHL

United Nations   Nations Unies
NEW YORK   GENÈVE

As the invisible planets that circle around the visible stars are thousands of light-years away, nobody from planet Earth will ever reach them alive by space craft. But a new electronic device substituting the present primitive telescope will enable our descendants to see life as it was on other planets thousands of years ago. And inside the atom and outside the universe we will discover the invisible creator of evolution.

© UNITED NATIONS

Tenerife,
Canary Islands
March, 1997

Address

Thor Heyerdahl

Thor Heyerdahl

As the invisible planets that circle around the visible stars are thousands of light-years away, nobody from planet Earth will ever reach them alive by space craft. But a new electronic device substituting the present primitive telescope will enable our descendants to see life as it was on other planets thousands of years ago. And inside the atom and outside the universe we will discover the invisible creator of evolution.

DR. RICHARD LEAKEY

Birthplace:
Nairobi, Kenya

Age at the Millennium: 56

Perhaps the world's most famous paleoanthropologist, Richard Leakey is the son of fellow scientists Louis and Mary. Leakey has continued to lead expeditions and publish essays, while also directing Kenya's Wildlife Service.

United Nations   Nations Unies
NEW YORK   GENÈVE

Well before the end of the Third Millennium, humans will have developed the ability to create self replicating, living biological entities using entirely artificial or non-natural biological means. This achievement of becoming a 'CREATOR' will have far reaching implications to deist centered belief systems where creation has been the basis for religious adherence. Theological thinking will fail to respond and the principal religions of the first and second millenniums will become no more than history.

Richard Leakey

MAY 8TH 1997

© UNITED NATIONS

Address

Richard Leakey

**Nairobi,
Kenya.**

♦   ♦   ♦   ♦   ♦

Walter Schirra is the third American to have orbited Earth, having piloted the *Mercury 8* orbital flight. He also piloted *Gemini 6*, the first spacecraft to rendezvous with another, and commanded *Apollo 7*, an eleven-day mission.

Birthplace:
Hackensack, N.J.

Age at the
Millennium: 77

CAPT. WALTER M. SCHIRRA

I left Earth three times, Mercury 8, Gemini 6 and Apollo 7, and I found no other place to live. Please take care of Spaceship Earth!

But, if during the next millennium, the earthlings work together new propulsion systems may permit terraforming Mars.

Good luck and commitment can provide wonders.

Wally Schirra

Capt. Walter M. SCHIRRA USN (Ret)

Address
Rancho Santa Fe, CA

8 June 1997

© UNITED NATIONS

I left Earth three times, Mercury 8, Gemini 6 and Apollo 7, and I found no other place to live. Please take care of Spaceship Earth!
But, if during the next millennium, the earthlings work together new propulsion systems may permit terraforming Mars.

Good luck and commitment can provide wonders.

BRIG. GEN. CHUCK YEAGER

Birthplace:
Myra, W.Va.

Age at the Millennium: 77

The first man to travel at the speed of sound, Chuck Yeager broke the sound barrier in 1947 at age 23. Breaking many other records, Yeager is the main character in Tom Wolfe's famous book *The Right Stuff* and he has become an American legend.

United Nations   Nations Unies
NEW YORK   GENÈVE

Men and Women will set foot on many of our Planets.

Chuck Yeager
T3/Gen USAF Ret
may 1, 1997
Grass Valley, Calif.

Address

©
UNITED
NATIONS

Men and women will set foot on many of our planets.

15 In 1967, Christiaan Barnard made world headlines by being the first to accomplish a successful human heart transplant. Criticized at first, the South African doctor later repeated the operation with greater success significantly advancing medical science.

Birthplace: Beaufort West, South Africa

Age at the Millennium: 78

DR. CHRISTIAAN BARNARD

United Nations   Nations Unies
NEW YORK   GENÈVE

The unrealistic expectations of Freedom and Rights will destroy the Western Civilisation, unless it is recognised that these ideals are priviliges and not necessities and therefore they are accompanied by responsibilities.

Maga 11, 1997

Address

©
UNITED
NATIONS

The unrealistic expectations of Freedom and Rights will destroy the Western Civilization unless it is recognised that these ideals are privileges and not necessities and therefore they are accompanied by responsibilities.

Photo by Archive Photos

RICHARD MEIER

Birthplace:
Chicago, Ill.

Age at the Millennium: 66

One of America's premier architects, Richard Meier is best known as the architect of the J. Paul Getty Art Museum in Los Angeles. Meier was only the sixth person to receive the Pritzker Prize, architecture's highest honor.

21

United Nations   Nations Unies
NEW YORK   GENÈVE

It is in the city where the discipline of architecture will still be urgently needed. there are issues in the city that only have an answer in architectural terms. Architecture will still be needed as the art of. architecture and necessity are still an issue.

Address

©
UNITED
NATIONS

It is in the city where the discipline of architecture will still be urgently needed. There are issues in the city that only have an answer in architectural terms. Architecture will still be needed as the art of architecture and necessity are still an issue.

Photo by Luca Vignelli

One of astronomy's leading stellar cartographers, it is believed that Margaret Geller has mapped more of the universe than any other individual. Geller has written for numerous science journals and works at the Harvard-Smithsonian Center for Astrophysics.

Birthplace:
Ithaca, N.Y.

Age at the Millennium: 53

DR. MARGARET J. GELLER

United Nations   Nations Unies
NEW YORK   GENÈVE

"We" will map the entire visible universe ... and we will understand the origin of planets, stars, galaxies ... and of the universe itself.

Margaret J. Geller

Cambridge MA USA
July 20, 1997

"We" will map the entire visible universe . . . and we will understand the origin of planets, stars, galaxies . . . and of the universe itself.

Photo by Roger Ressmeyer / © Corbis

DR. JAMES A. VAN ALLEN

Birthplace:
Mount Pleasant, Iowa

**Age at the
Millennium:** 86

A major astronomical physicist of the century, James Van Allen discovered the radiation particles around Earth now known as Van Allen belts. Van Allen was also the chief investigator of most early American space probes.

218

United Nations   Nations Unies
NEW YORK   GENÈVE

During the Third Millennium:

1) I expect marked improvements in human health care, including the reduction of genetically based disabilities — physical and mental.

2) I do not expect human space flight to become commonplace.

James G. Van Allen

©
UNITED
NATIONS

Iowa City   1/18/98

During the Third Millennium:

1) I expect marked improvements in human health care, including the reduction of genetically based disabilities—physical and mental.

2) I do not expect human space flight to become commonplace.

Director of the SETI Institute, Frank Drake heads the most serious organization seeking to confirm extraterrestrial life. An astronomer, Drake pioneered the search for nonhuman radio signals while heading the world's largest radio telescope at Arecibo, Puerto Rico.

Birthplace:
Chicago, Ill.

**Age at the
Millennium: 70**

DR. FRANK DRAKE

A prediction for the next millennium:

We will discover other intelligent civilizations in space. We will learn much from them; information which will motivate us, enrich our spirit, and make life better for all humanity

Address

Frank Drake
SETI Institute
Mountain View
California
December 31, 1997

©
UNITED
NATIONS

A prediction for the next millennium: We will discover other intelligent civilizations in space. We will learn much from them; information which will motivate us, enrich our spirit, and make life better for all humanity.

Photo by Reuters/Lou Dematteis/Archive Photos

DR. HENRY C. LEE

Birthplace: Jiangsu, China

Age at the Millennium: 62

One of the world's leading forensic scientists, Henry C. Lee has investigated more than 5,000 cases. Technically with the Connecticut State Police, his expertise is sought by hundreds of law enforcement agencies each year.

United Nations   Nations Unies
NEW YORK   GENÈVE

We will be blessed in an age where microchip technology has reached a plateau and enter into a burgeoning golden era where the scientific community can apply itself to realizing the full potential of this technology. Rapid identification and individualization systems will be commonplace, as will expert systems. These will be the new tools for tomorrow's investigator.

DR. HENRY C. LEE
Director, Professor
Connecticut State Police
Forensic Science Laboratory
Meriden, Connecticut

Address   **Todd W. Nickerson**

Millennium Committee of
   New York, LLC
Box 20292
Dag Hammarskjold P.C.C.
New York, NY   10017-0003

©
UNITED
NATIONS

The third American in space, Alan Bean followed Alan Shepard and John Glenn. He later commanded *Apollo 12*, becoming the third man to step onto the Moon. Bean also served as commander on *Skylab*.

Birthplace:
Wheeler, Tex.

Age at the
Millennium: 68

CAPT. ALAN
BEAN

United Nations   Nations Unies
NEW YORK   GENÈVE

BETWEEN THE YEARS 2001-3000 CITIES WILL BE BUILT IN ORBIT AROUND PLANET EARTH, ON THE MOON AND ON MARS. MILLIONS OF HUMANS WILL LIVE AND WORK THERE IN PEACE.

Alan Bean
APOLLO 12 ASTRONAUT
1 JUNE 1997

Address

©
UNITED
NATIONS

Between the years 2001–3000 cities will be built in orbit around planet Earth, on the Moon and on Mars. Millions of humans will live and work there in peace.

WILSON GREATBATCH

Birthplace:
Buffalo, N.Y.

Age at the Millennium: 81

The inventor of the implantable cardiac pacemaker, Wilson Greatbatch is credited with saving numerous lives from heart disease. His company remains a market leader in the pacemaker industry.

United Nations   Nations Unies
NEW YORK   GENÈVE

1. THE COMPLETELY IMPLANTABLE MECHANICAL HEART WILL BECOME AVAILABLE AND COMMONLY USED.

2. MOST ELECTRICAL POWER WILL COME FROM SMALL LOCAL PLANTS, DERIVED FROM NUCLEAR FUSION OF HELIUM-3 WHICH WE WILL OBTAIN FROM THE MOON. THE FUEL WILL BE RADIATION-FREE, THE PROCESS WILL BE RADIATION-FREE, AND THE RESIDUE WILL BE RADIATION-FREE.

3. COMMUNICATION WILL BE INSTANTANEOUS, WORLD-WIDE. EVERYONE IN THE WORLD WILL BE IN INSTANT COMMUNICATION WITH EVERYONE ELSE BY SATELLITE/CELLULAR PHONE.

Wilson Greatbatch

UNITED NATIONS

(Inventor of the Implantable Cardiac Pacemaker)
27 MAY 1997

---

1. The completely implantable mechanical heart will become available and commonly used.

2. Most electrical power will come from small local plants, derived from nuclear fusion of helium-3, which we will obtain from the moon. The fuel will be radiation-free, the process will be radiation-free, and the residue will be radiation-free.

3. Communication will be instantaneous, world-wide. Everyone in the world will be in instant communication with everyone else by satellite/cellular phone.

223 Jake Garn made history in 1985 when, as a sitting U.S. senator, he joined the crew of the space shuttle *Discovery* and became an astronaut. A former navy pilot, his subcommittee oversaw NASA. Garn is an avid proponent of the shuttle program.

Birthplace:
Richfield, Utah

Age at the Millennium: 68

JAKE GARN

United Nations   Nations Unies
NEW YORK   GENÈVE

MEN AND WOMEN WILL STAND ON THE SURFACE OF MARS IN THE FIRST HALF OF THE NEXT CENTURY. I ALSO BELIEVE WE WILL DISCOVER THAT INTELLIGENT LIFE EXISTS IN THE UNIVERSE. WE ARE NOT ALONE!

Jake Garn
US SENATOR UTAH
1974 - 1993
SPACE SHUTTLE DISCOVERY
APRIL 1985

SALT LAKE CITY
1997

Address

©
UNITED
NATIONS

Men and women will stand on the surface of Mars in the first half of the next century. I also believe we will discover that intelligent life exists in the universe. We are not alone!

DR. LAURA SCHLESSINGER

Birthplace:
New York, N.Y.

Age at the Millennium: 52

The most famous psychiatrist on radio, Laura Schlessinger's syndicated talk show reaches an estimated fifteen million listeners weekly. Schlessinger dispenses advice that emphasizes accountability and ethical choices, particularly for family matters.

22

United Nations   Nations Unies
NEW YORK   GENÈVE

I am hopeful that people will put G-d and family before their own selfish interests and desires.

Laura Schlessinger

Address

UNITED NATIONS

I am hopeful that people will put God and family before their own selfish interests and desires.

As manager of NASA's Mars Exploration Program, Donna Shirley headed the team that planned the *Pathfinder* mission and landed the *Sojourner* rover on Mars on July 4, 1997. Shirley has worked at the Jet Propulsion Laboratory since 1966.

Birthplace:
Wynnewood, Okla.

Age at the Millennium: 59

DONNA L. SHIRLEY

United Nations · Nations Unies
NEW YORK · GENÈVE

3/27/98

LA CANADA, CALIFORNIA

• Discovery of past life on Mars by 2016.

• 1st humans on Mars by 2025

• Self sustaining colony on Mars by 2100.

DONNA L. SHIRLEY
MANAGER, MARS EXPLORATION PROGRAM
JET PROPULSION LABORATORY
CALIFORNIA INSTITUTE OF TECHNOLOGY

Address

UNITED NATIONS

• *Discovery of past life on Mars by 2016.*
• *1st humans on Mars by 2025.*
• *Self-sustaining colony on Mars by 2100.*

DR. ROBERT BALLARD

Birthplace:
Abilene, Kans.

**Age at the
Millennium: 58**

Best known as the scientist who found the wreckage of the RMS *Titanic*, the *Bismarck*, and the *Lusitania*, Robert Ballard has redefined the field of marine archeology with his careful research of ancient ships. Ballard also directs the Center for Marine Exploration.

United Nations   Nations Unies
NEW YORK   GENÈVE

My prediction is as follows:

I believe that during the next Millennium undersea explorers will find numerous lost chapters in human history that will greatly alter our thoughts and theories about the movement and trade between humans in ancient times.

Robert D. Ballard, Ph.D.
President, The Institute for Exploration
Mystic, Connecticut
April 21, 1998

©
UNITED
NATIONS

227 The best chess player in the world, Garry Kasparov became the youngest champion in history at age 22. Now the longest-reigning champion (since 1985), Kasparov is a national icon in his homeland of Russia.

**Birthplace:
Baku, Azerbaijan**

**Age at the
Millennium: 37**

GARRY KASPAROV

United Nations   Nations Unies
NEW YORK   GENÈVE

From cyberspace to outer space. Conquer and cultivate!

Address

©
UNITED
NATIONS

From cyberspace to outer space. Conquer and cultivate!

CAPT. DON WALSH

Birthplace:
Berkeley, Calif.

**Age at the
Millennium: 69**

As commander of the submarine that holds the world's dive record, Don Walsh joined explorer Jacques Piccard to the deepest point ever reached by man (35,800 ft. below sea level), the Marianas Trench. Walsh's ship, *Trieste-I,* is now a navy museum.

United Nations   Nations Unies
NEW YORK   GENÈVE

I am an oceans person... I believe oceanspace is every bit as important as outer space, if not more so. My prediction for Third Millennium is that finally the peoples of the world will recognize the critical importance of the oceans to our collective well-being on this planet. The result will be major global investments of public will and funding to explore and study the seas.

In this next century, most of us will live out our lives confined to 'Spaceship Earth'. The health of the world ocean determines our viability as a civilization. Properly used, its resources can help supply the needs of a rapidly increasing world population. However, the world ocean is downhill from virtually all of man's activities and adverse changes here are subtle and often irreversible. Once apparent, it may be too late to reverse these changes.

Let's not foul our nest. We did not care very well for the oceans in the past. If we do nothing now, they will not care for us in the Third Millennium.

Don Walsh

©
UNITED
NATIONS

The sixth man to walk on the Moon, Edgar Mitchell accompanied Alan Shepard aboard *Apollo 14*'s lunar landing. After retiring, Mitchell founded the Institute of Noetic Sciences, controversially exploring extraterrestrial investigations.

Birthplace:
Hereford, Tex.

Age at the
Millennium: 70

DR. EDGAR MITCHELL

United Nations   Nations Unies
NEW YORK   GENÈVE

If humankind will confront and solve the problems of the late 20th Century such as overpopulation, ecological destruction, and a runaway consumer economics, it likely can have an enduring future. Civilization at the turn of the millennium is not on a sustainable path and the present challenge is to create one for the betterment of all species.

©
UNITED NATIONS

Address

Edgar Mitchell
Astronaut, Apollo 14
1997 Palm Beach, Florida USA.

If humankind will confront and solve the problems of the late 20th century such as overpopulation, ecological destruction, and a runaway consumer economics, it likely can have an enduring future. Civilization at the turn of the millennium is not on a sustainable path and the present challenge is to create one for the betterment of all species.

SHARON MATOLA

Birthplace:
Baltimore, Md.

Age at the
Millennium: 46

As the founder of the Belize Zoo and Tropical Education Center, Sharon Matola established one of the most authentic tropical habitats in the world. Matola has received wide praise for encouraging environmental awareness among native Central Americans.

United Nations Nations Unies
NEW YORK GENÈVE

14 JAN 1998
THE BELIZE ZOO & TROPICAL EDUCATION CENTER
MILE 29   WESTERN HWY.
BELIZE, CENTRAL AMERICA

Address

TO THE MILLENNIUM Committee:
I believe that an important event will continue to happen
in the next millennium:
   Migratory Birds will still be Migrating

~ which means we will have wisely
   preserved the necessary habitat
   for the continuation of this incredible event —

©
UNITED
NATIONS

Sharon Matola

I believe that an important event will continue to happen in the next millennium: Migratory birds will still be migrating.

—Which means we will have wisely preserved the necessary habitat for the continuation of this incredible event—

President of the Sierra Club, Adam Werbach is the youngest person to ever head a major environmental group in the United States. With 600,000 members, Werbach oversees the group's budget, lobbying, and conservation efforts.

Birthplace:
North Hollywood, Calif.

Age at the Millennium: 27

ADAM WERBACH

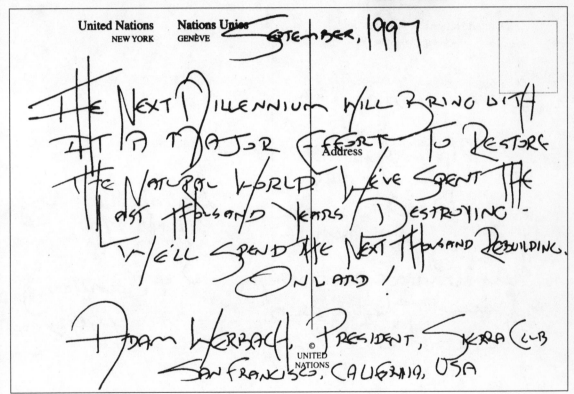

The next millennium will bring with it a major effort to restore the natural world. We've spent the last thousand years destroying. We'll spend the next thousand rebuilding. Onward!

DR. DAVID H. LEVY

Birthplace:
Montreal, Canada

Age at the Millennium: 52

Codiscoverer of Comet Shoemaker-Levy 9, David Levy is among the world's foremost comet hunters with over twenty discoveries. The Shoemaker-Levy comet's dramatic collision with Jupiter in 1994 is considered one of the most important astronomical events ever observed.

23

United Nations   Nations Unies

NEW YORK   GENÈVE

It is my hope that the people of this world will see our planet as one of many, and that they will appreciate at last the value of other worlds in space.

Address

*David H. Levy
Vail, Az.
24 January
1998*

UNITED NATIONS

It is my hope that the people of this world will see our planet as one of many, and that they will appreciate at last the value of other worlds in space.

Photo by Wendee Wallach-Levy

233 The designer of the 747 airplane, Joseph Sutter revolutionized the airline industry by proving that a wide-bodied civilian jet airliner could be technically and economically feasible. Sutter headed the aerodynamics development for Boeing's entire 707 family.

Birthplace:
Seattle, Wash.

Age at the Millennium: 79

JOSEPH SUTTER

WHERE WILL WE BE, AS A CIVILIZATION, IN THE YEAR 3000. IT DEPENDS ON US. WE LEARN TO LIVE TOGETHER & TOGETHER WORK TO PROTECT OUR ENVIRNOMENT. WE ALSO USE THE CONTINUOUS EVOLVING TECHNOLOGIES TO SUPPORT THIS EFFORT, NUCULAR & SOLAR ENERGY WILL REPLACE FOSSIL FUELS AS OUR MAJOR SOURCE OF POWER. WE WILL EXPLORE THE UNIVERSE — BUT WE WILL CONTINUE TO INHABIT THIS EARTH OF OURS. WE HAVE TO DO THIS. THE ALTERATIVE DOES NOT BARE THINKING ABOUT

Address JOE SUTTER *
SEATTLE, WASHINGTON

AUGUST 5, 1997

* DESIGNER OF THE BOEING 747 AIRPLANE

Where will we be, as a civilization, in the year 3000. It depends on us. We learn to live together and together work to protect our environment. We also use the continuous evolving technologies to support this effort, nuclear and solar energy will replace fossil fuels as our major source of power. We will explore the universe—but we will continue to inhabit this Earth of ours. We have to do this. The alternative does not bear thinking about.

DR. HARRISON H. SCHMITT

Birthplace:
Santa Rita, N.Mex.

Age at the Millennium: 65

The only civilian or scientist to set foot on the Moon, Harrison Schmitt holds a Ph.D. in geology from Harvard. His *Apollo 17* mission was mankind's last landing on the Moon in the twentieth century. Schmitt was later elected to the U.S. Senate.

United Nations Nations Unies
NEW YORK GENÈVE

Early in the next millennium, the fusion energy resources (^{3}He) of the Moon will enable (1) the alleviation of increased energy demand on Earth, and its related social and environmental consequences, (2) the establishment of self-sufficient enclaves of the human species on the Moon and Mars, (3) the preservation of human freedom at the new frontiers of space as well as on Earth, and (4) the movement of humans into the vast reaches of the Milky Way Galaxy.

Harrison H. Schmitt

Address

©
UNITED
NATIONS

Harrison H. Schmitt
Geologist, Ph.D.
Apollo 17 Astronaut
United States
Senator (R-NM)
Businessman

Known as the "Father of the Internet," Vinton Cerf coinvented the Internet's TCP/IP communications protocol. The founding president of the Internet Society and a speaker sought worldwide, Cerf is senior vice president of Data Services Architecture at MCI.

Birthplace:
New Haven, Conn.

Age at the
Millennium: 57

DR. VINTON CERF

United Nations   Nations Unies
NEW YORK   GENÈVE

By 2025 Internet will be interplanetary in scope. We will have colonies on the moon and mars. Interstellar probes will have been launched. By 2400, we will have multiple manned missions to other star systems. Bioelectronics will heal and improve upon our natural senses. Artificial intelligence will be a reality. New species, adapted for new environments, will have been created. By 3000, we will have solved the limitations of light speed.

Address

© UNITED NATIONS

Vint Cerf

By 2025 Internet will be interplanetary in scope. We will have colonies on the moon and mars. Interstellar probes will have been launched. By 2400, we will have multiple manned missions to other star systems. Bioelectronics will heal and improve upon our natural senses. Artificial intelligence will be a reality. New species, adapted for new environments, will have been created. By 3000, we will have solved the limitations of light speed.

CAPT. EUGENE CERNAN

Birthplace:
Chicago, Ill.

**Age at the
Millennium: 66**

The last person to have stepped from the surface of the Moon, Eugene Cernan commanded *Apollo 17*, NASA's final lunar mission. Cernan also piloted earlier Gemini and Apollo missions, laying the groundwork for Neil Armstrong's landing.

United Nations   Nations Unies
NEW YORK   GENÈVE

The legacy of Apollo will carry us on to Mars early in the next Millennium—and then who knows where!

Chapter 9

Sports

Birthplace: Placentia, Calif.

Age at the Millennium: 29

The most famous female swimmer in the United States, Janet Evans stunned the sports world by earning three gold medals in the 1988 Seoul Olympics. Evans earned further medals in 1992 and 1996 and has won over seventy national championships.

United Nations NEW YORK   **Nations Unies** GENÈVE

What will happen in the next millenium? As an athlete, I believe that every four years the Olympics will continue to represent athletes at their best. And on a much larger scale, I believe that the people of this world will continue to do their best in everything they do.

No one knows what the future will hold, and predictions only sometimes come true. In the next millenium, I believe that we might make major advancements in technology, we might have some conflicts and disagreements and we might be continued to be amazed by Mother Nature's powers. But I know just one thing: regardless of the above mentioned events, all of mankind will forever demonstrate their spirit, kindness, determination and desire to succeed, just like athletes do in the Olympics.

Janet Evans, Los Angeles 1997

UNITED NATIONS ©

What will happen in the next millennium? As an athlete, I believe that every four years the Olympics will continue to represent athletes at their best. And on a much larger scale, I believe that the people of this world will continue to do their best in everything they do.

No one knows what the future will hold, and predictions only sometimes come true. In the next millennium, I believe that we might make major advancements in technology. We might have some conflicts and disagreements and we might be continued to be amazed by Mother Nature's powers. But I know just one thing: regardless of the above mentioned events, all of mankind will forever demonstrate their spirit, kindness, determination and desire to succeed, just like athletes do in the Olympics.

One of the most popular figure skaters ever, Kurt Browning competed in three winter Olympics and broke several records. Browning was named Canadian Athlete of the Year several times between 1988 and 1994, and now skates professionally.

Birthplace:
Caroline, Canada

Age at the Millennium: 34

KURT BROWNING

United Nations   Nations Unies
NEW YORK   GENÈVE

Hello to the World,

Since sports have been a part of my life since before I can remember, I will make a guess as to the future of the Olympics. Every year new sports are being added. Soon the Olympics will just be too big and confusing.

Maybe the Olympics will have to divide with one "Games" devoted to the more traditional sports while the modern "Games" will host all the new events. I guess they could be called the Extreme Olympics.

Flying Skates ??

Back here in 1997, Canada is a great place to live. I hope that this continues.

Address

Be good to each other and drive ... whatever you all drive now? ... drive it safely.

Yours,

Kurt Browning

© UNITED NATIONS

Hello to the World,
Since sports have been a part of my life since before I can remember, I will make a guess as to the future of the Olympics. Every year new sports are being added. Soon the Olympics will just be too big and confusing.
Maybe the Olympics will have to divide with one "Games" devoted to the more traditional sports while the modern "Games" will host all the new events. I guess they could be called the Extreme Olympics.

Flying Skates??
Back here in 1997, Canada is a great place to live. I hope that this continues.
Be good to each other and drive . . . whatever you all drive now? . . . drive it safely.

GARY PLAYER

Birthplace: Johannesburg, South Africa

Age at the Millennium: 65

Gary Player is one of only four persons to win the four Grand Slam events of golf, and was the first non-American to win the U.S. Open in forty-five years. Player is now a horse breeder in South Africa.

United Nations **Nations Unies**
NEW YORK   GENÈVE

1. We will fly commercially from N.Y. to South Africa in under two hours.

2. People will visit and live on other planets.

3. Human cloning and gene splicing will be common place.

4. Jesus Christ will return to rule for a 1000 years.

Gary Player, South Africa, Jan 1998.

---

1. We will fly commercially from N.Y. to South Africa in under two hours.

2. People will visit and live on other planets.

3. Human cloning and gene splicing will be common place.

4. Jesus Christ will return to rule for 1000 years.

Long considered the greatest hockey player alive, Gordie Howe played in the NHL for over thirty years. His record for goals scored was only recently surpassed by Wayne Gretzky. Howe and his wife, Colleen, are known as Mr. & Mrs. Hockey®.

Birthplace:
Saskatoon, Canada

Age at the Millennium: 72

GORDIE AND COLLEEN HOWE

United Nations   **Nations Unies**
NEW YORK   GENÈVE

As we approach the millennium . . .

My prediction is that the medical profession will find the skill to no longer have to invade the human body in order to cure illnesses like cancer. Surgery, as we know it, will be thought of as barbaric.

Address

I predict there will be a lady with one of the N.H.L. teams in the near future.

MARIO ANDRETTI

Birthplace:
Montona, Italy

Age at the Millennium: 60

One of the greatest race car drivers ever, Mario Andretti is the only person to have won the Grand Prix, the Daytona 500, and the Indianapolis 500. Andretti has won sixteen Grand Prix in his Formula One career.

United Nations   Nations Unies
NEW YORK   GENÈVE

I predict there will be auto racing on Mars before the year 3000.

Address

Mario Andretti
Nazareth, Pa.

Feb. 1, 1998

©
UNITED
NATIONS

I predict there will be auto racing on Mars before the year 3000.

The last Hall of Fame Brooklyn Dodger, Pee Wee Reese starred during the 1940s and 1950s, including Brooklyn's famous World Series win in 1954. Reese briefly played and coached for the Dodgers following their fateful move to Los Angeles.

Birthplace:
Ekron, N.Y.

Age at the Millennium: 82

PEE WEE REESE

United Nations   Nations Unies
NEW YORK   GENÈVE

1/10/98

I believe that between the years 2001 to 3000 the black race and the white race will become as one, all american, I hope and pray this is true. This was also the dream of Jackie Robinson.

Address

Pee Wee Reese

©
UNITED
NATIONS

I believe that between the years 2001 to 3000 the black race and the
white race will become as one, all American, I hope and pray this is true.
This was also the dream of Jackie Robinson.

LYNN SWANN

Birthplace:
Alcoa, Tenn.

Age at the
Millennium: 48

One of the best receivers in NFL history, Lynn Swann helped his Pittsburgh Steelers to four Super Bowl wins. A Hall of Fame and All-Time NFL team member, Swann has broadcasted for ABC since 1976.

United Nations   Nations Unies
NEW YORK   GENÈVE

From the year 2001 To 3000 I predict that we will insure that every child will be given the tools and chance to succeed in life. Regardless of color, financial position or physical ability or disability we will find a way, create the program and most importantly, make the effort.

Address

Lynn Swann
Pittsburgh, Pa.
June 24, 1997

© UNITED NATIONS

From the year 2001 to 3000 I predict that we will insure that every child will be given the tools and chance to succeed in life. Regardless of color, financial position or physical ability or disability we will find a way, create the program and most importantly, make the effort.

A basketball legend, Bob Cousy played for the Boston Celtics from 1950 to 1963. Cousy led the Celtics to six N.B.A. titles over seven years, and was inducted into the Hall of Fame in 1970.

Birthplace:
New York, N.Y.

Age at the Millennium: 72

BOB COUSY

United Nations **Nations Unies**
NEW YORK GENÈVE

[handwritten message]

Address

©
UNITED
NATIONS

I believe inter-planetary travel will become commonplace with stations and even settlements established. Hopefully contact and communication with other life forms in a peaceful way. Perhaps some may even become basketball players, in which case the N.B.A. can truly expand.

SHANNON MILLER

Birthplace:
Rollo, Mo.

Age at the Millennium: 23

One of America's best Olympic gymnasts, Shannon Miller received the silver medal in 1992 and gold medal in 1996 for her individual balance beam performances. Miller also greatly contributed to the team gold medal given to the United States in 1996.

United Nations   Nations Unies
NEW YORK   GENÈVE

I believe scientists could find a cure for diseases such as Aids and Cancer in the next millennium.

I am also looking forward to the advances in technology leading to the building of colonies in space.

Shannon Miller
gymnast

Address

© UNITED NATIONS

I believe scientists could find a cure for diseases such as Aids and Cancer in the next millennium.

I am also looking forward to the advances in technology leading to the building of colonies in space.

Photo by Reuters / Wolfgang Rattay / Archive Photos

Named U.S. Basketball Coach of the Year for four years, Mike Krzyzewski is one of the most popular figures in college sports. Krzyzewski is known for his scandal-free teams at Duke, and for tying John Wooden's record in 1992 with back-to-back NCAA titles.

Birthplace:
Chicago, Ill.

Age at the Millennium: 53

MIKE KRZYZEWSKI

United Nations   Nations Unies
NEW YORK   GENÈVE

"DIVERSITY". We will learn to embrace it, instead of fearing it! As a result, we will find a way of life "for all" that no one could have imagined. Once we TRUST one another, there will be no limits!

© UNITED NATIONS

Address

Mike Krzyzewski

11 August, 1997
Durham, North Carolina
DUKE UNIVERSITY

"DIVERSITY"——We will learn to embrace it, instead of fearing it! As a result, we will find a way of life "for all" that no one could have imagined.
Once we TRUST one another, there will be no limits!

OLGA KORBUT

Birthplace:
Grodno, Belarus

Age at the
Millennium: 44

Despite the Cold War, Olga Korbut's gold medal gymnastics performances during the 1972 Olympics earned her admiration in both her native USSR and the USA. Her following began the subsequent following of gymnastics as a spectator sport.

United Nations   Nations Unies
NEW YORK   GENÈVE

OLGA KORBUT
ATLANTA

Address

Хацела б
незалежнасці
маёй краіне
Беларусь ад
камуністаў
маскалёў і
дурняў!
Міру і шчасця
ўсім усіх народаў!

Olga Korbut

©
UNITED
NATIONS

I would like to see my country, Belarus, independent from Communists, Russian low-life soldiers and the idiots. Peace and happiness for all nations.

249 In seventeen seasons, Earl Weaver coached his Baltimore Orioles to four World Series. Despite a record ninety-eight ejections, Weaver retired with the sixteenth-best all-time coaching record and was inducted into the Hall of Fame.

Birthplace:
Saint Louis, Mo.

Age at the Millennium: 70

EARL WEAVER

United Nations   Nations Unies
NEW YORK   **GENÈVE**

I PREDICT THAT THE CHICAGO CUBS, AND BOSTON RED SOX BASEBALL TEAMS WILL BOTH WIN A WORLD CHAMPIONSHIP BEFORE THE YEAR 2500

Earl Weaver
Pembroke Pines FL.
May 31, 1997

Address

©
UNITED
NATIONS

I predict that the Chicago Cubs and Boston Red Sox baseball teams will both win a world championship before the year 2,500.

Photo by Archive Photos

MIKE DITKA

Birthplace: Carnegie, Pa.

Age at the Millennium: 61

One of the most famous personalities in the NFL, Mike Ditka began his football career as the 1961 Rookie of the Year with the Chicago Bears. Ditka played for eleven years before taking up coaching, running the Bears for over a decade.

United Nations   Nations Unies
NEW YORK   GENÈVE

THE U.S.A. HAS BECOME THE GREATEST NATION ON EARTH, BECAUSE OF IT'S PEOPLE.

PEOPLE FROM ALL RACE'S, CREED'S AND RELIGIONS WORKING TO BETTER THEM SELVES AND THEIR FAMILIES.

WE MUST EDUCATE OUR YOUTH TO DO WHAT IS RIGHT IN THE EYE'S OF GOD IF WE ARE TO CONTINUE TO GROW & PROSPER.

Address

Mike Ditka

N.O. LOUISIANA.
4/24/97

© UNITED NATIONS

The U.S.A. has become the greatest nation on Earth, because of its people. People from all races, creeds and religions working to better themselves and their families. We must educate our youth to do what is right in the eyes of God if we are to continue to grow and prosper.

251 One of the most popular basketball
commentators in the sport, Tom Heinsohn
previously was with the Boston Celtics as both
player and coach (1956–1978). Heinsohn was
inducted into the Basketball Hall of Fame in
1985.

Birthplace:
Jersey City, N.J.

**Age at the
Millennium: 66**

TOM HEINSOHN

United Nations   Nations Unies
NEW YORK   GENÈVE

1. TELECOMMUNICATIONS WILL
DO AWAY WITH NATIONAL
BOUNDRIES AND SHOW PEOPLE
THEY HAVE MORE IN COMMON
THAN THEY HAVE DIFFER-
ENCES.

2. SPORTS WILL BE PLAYED
BY ROBOTS. THESE GAMES
WILL INVOLVE MORE
VIOLENCE THAN NOW.

Tom Heinsoh

TOM HEINSOHN 1997
NEWTON, MASS U.S.A.

3. MEDICINE WILL NEED TO
DEFEAT MAN'S BIGGEST
ENEMY, THE VIRUS.

4. HUMANS WILL LIVE
ON OTHER PLANETS.

Address

5. THE WONDERS OF
SPACE WILL SPARK
A NEW PHILOSOPHY.

6. HUMANS WILL BE
FORCED TO LIVE IN
A MORE STERILE
PROTECTED INVIRONMENT.

(c)
UNITED
NATIONS

---

1. Telecommunications will do away with national boundaries and
show people they have more in common than they have differences.

2. Sports will be played by robots. These games will involve more
violence than now.

3. Medicine will need to defeat man's biggest enemy, the virus.

4. Humans will live on other planets.

5. The wonders of space will spark a new philosophy.

6. Humans will be forced to live in a more sterile protected
environment.

TOM LASORDA

Birthplace: Norristown, Pa.

Age at the Millennium: 73

One of the most popular names in baseball, Tom Lasorda epitomizes the Dodgers and California baseball. Having coached the Dodgers for over twenty years with numerous pennants, Lasorda was inducted into the Hall of Fame in 1997.

United Nations   Nations Unies
NEW YORK   GENÈVE

I beleive that sometime between 2000 & the year 3000, that the world Series well become a real World Series, with Countries like Japan China, & Korea! I also beleive that the U.S.A well be the first to have transportation to the moon. May the world be a United World.

Good luck

Tom Lasorda V.P. of the Los Angeles Dodgers and former manager of twenty years

5-15-97

© UNITED NATIONS

I believe that sometime between 2000 & the year 3000, that the World Series will become a real World Series, with countries like Japan, China and Korea. I also believe that the U.S.A. will be the first to have transportation to the moon. May the world be a United World.
Good Luck.

Photo by Reuters / Sam Mircovich / Archive Photos

253 Norway's most famous athlete, Grete Waitz is known for her repeated victories in the New York City Marathon, winning nine times between 1978 and 1988. A silver medalist in the Olympics, Waitz holds numerous marathon records.

Birthplace:
Oslo, Norway

Age at the Millennium: 47

GRETE WAITZ

It is my prediction -
my hope - that in the most
developed nations on earth,
generations of the next millennium
will gain the wisdom to take
power over their own lives
and experience the joys and
benefits of physical fitness
and good health.

Address

Grete Waitz

Marathon Champion.

©
UNITED
NATIONS

It is my prediction—my hope—that in the most developed nations on earth, generations of the next millennium will gain the wisdom to take power over their own lives, and experience the joys and benefits of physical fitness and good health.

Photo by Reuters / Ray Stubblebine / Archive Photos

LENNY WILKENS

Birthplace:
New York, N.Y.

Age at the Millennium: 63

The winningest head coach in NBA history, Lenny Wilkens has won over 1,000 games in twenty-four seasons. He also coached the gold-medal 1996 Olympic "Dream Team." Wilkens continues to build on his record as coach of the Atlanta Hawks.

United Nations　　Nations Unies
NEW YORK　　GENÈVE

Address

Power Source will be at its Peak or will decline.
Technology — Transportation
AT ITS Best.
CURES FOR CANCER + AIDS

Lenny Wilkens — Atlanta, Ga. 1997

UNITED NATIONS

Power source will be at its peak or will decline. Technology—transportation at its best. Cures for Cancer and AIDS.

Marv Levy, a Harvard graduate, coached numerous college teams prior to becoming head coach of the Kansas City Chiefs in 1978 and later the Buffalo Bills. The only NFL coach to appear in four consecutive Super Bowls, Levy retired in 1998.

Birthplace:
Chicago, Ill.

Age at the
Millennium: 71

MARV LEVY

United Nations   Nations Unies
NEW YORK   GENÈVE

Sometime during this next millennium I believe that we, here on Earth, will have contact with and will communicate with intelligent life elsewhere in this universe.

Marv Levy
Head Coach - Buffalo Bills

Orchard Park, New York
June 23, 1997

©
UNITED
NATIONS

Sometime during the next millennium I believe that we, here on Earth, will have contact with and will communicate with intelligent life elsewhere in this universe.

Photo by Reuters / Joe Traver / Archive Photos

NADIA COMANECI

Birthplace:
Onesti, Moldova

**Age at the
Millennium: 39**

Nadia Comaneci became the first Olympic gymnast in history to score a perfect 10, earning seven gold medals in 1976. A hero in Romania, Comaneci's 1989 defection to the United States was a major news event.

United Nations   Nations Unies
NEW YORK   GENÈVE

Between 2001 - 3000 will be no more wars and people will have a happier life.

Address

Norman, OK

© UNITED NATIONS

Between 2001–3000 will be no more wars and people will have a
happier life.

257 A legendary Hall of Fame football player of the 1940s and 1950s, Otto Graham was rated the NFL's best passer for six years of his ten-year career. Graham led his Cleveland Browns to seven championship seasons.

Birthplace:
Waukegan, Ill.

Age at the Millennium: 79

OTTO GRAHAM

United Nations   Nations Unies
NEW YORK   GENÈVE

2001-3000

IF HUMANity IS To SURVIVE THE NEXT MILLENNIUM WE MUST LEARN TO EMBRACE AND RESPECT OUR ENVIRONMENT, CELEBRATE OUR SPIRITUAL DIFFERENCES, AND CREATE A TOMORROW WHERE BIAS AND COLOR ARE A NON-ISSUE

Otto Graham

Address

©
UNITED
NATIONS

If humanity is to survive the next millennium we must learn to embrace and respect our environment, celebrate our spiritual differences, and create a tomorrow where bias and color are a non-issue.

GREG NORMAN

Birthplace:
Mount Isa, Australia

Age at the
Millennium: 45

Australia's most famous golfer, Greg Norman has won over fifty tournaments and has been a dominant presence in the sport since the 1980s. Norman has also achieved great success in the business world, leading several highly successful golf-related enterprises.

United Nations Nations Unies
NEW YORK   GENÈVE

CURE FOR ALL
ILLNESS

Address

©
UNITED
NATIONS

Cure for all illness

Photo by Popperfoto / Archive Photos

259   Considered to be baseball's most distinguished broadcaster, Tim McCarver had a twenty-one year career as a player before retiring in 1980. He immediately took up sportscasting. After fifteen years, McCarver left CBS for the Fox network.

Birthplace:
Memphis, Tenn.

Age at the
Millennium: 57

TIM McCARVER

United Nations   Nations Unies
NEW YORK   GENÈVE

1) BY THE YEAR 2050, HUMAN CLONING WITH CATASTROPHIC INITIAL RESULTS...
2) BY THE YEAR 2080, THE WORLD WILL BE HELD HOSTAGE BY A TERRORIST GROUP OR GROUPS WITH NUCLEAR CAPABILITIES...
3) PASSENGER TRIPS TO MARS BY THE YEAR 2200...
4) WITH THE DIMINISHING OF THE WORLD'S CHLOROPHIL AND OXYGEN IN THE ATMOSPHERE, STORMS (TORNADOES + HURRICANES) WITH 400-500 MPH WINDS WILL LEVEL WHOLE SECTIONS OF THE U.S. AND MEXICO
5) BY 2100, CHINA WILL BE THE WORLD'S NUMBER ONE POWER BY FAR...ASIAN POPULATION WILL REPRESENT 72% OF WORLD POPULATION

Tim McCarver

Address

TIM McCARVER

GLADWYNE, PA.
JUNE 2, 1999

©
UNITED
NATIONS

---

1. By the year 2050, human cloning with catastrophic initial results . . .
2. By the year 2080, the world will be held hostage by a terrorist group or groups with nuclear capabilities . . .
3. Passenger trips to Mars by the year 2200 . . .
4. With the diminishing of the world's chlorophil and oxygen in the atmosphere, storms (tornadoes and hurricanes) with 400–500 mph winds will level whole sections of the U.S. and Mexico.
5. By 2100, China will be the world's number one power by far . . . Asian population will represent 72% of world population.

Photo by FOX

JOE THEISMANN

Birthplace:
New Brunswick, N.J.

Age at the Millennium: 51

One of the Washington Redskin's greatest quarterbacks, Joe Theismann led his team to play-off games from 1979 to 1986, including one Super Bowl win. Theismann has been an outspoken sports commentator on ESPN since 1988.

United Nations   Nations Unies
NEW YORK   GENÈVE

Address

©
UNITED
NATIONS

Between 2001—3000 one of the great get-a-ways will be to spend time on a space station. At first the cost will be high but as time moves on it will become less expensive. Also, I'll be a grandfather.

The first person to win a gold medal in four consecutive Olympics (1956 to 1968), Al Oerter broke his own discus-throwing record each time. No other athlete has so dominated his sport for so long a period of time.

Birthplace:
New York, N.Y.

Age at the Millennium: 64

AL OERTER

United Nations   Nations Unies
NEW YORK   GENÈVE

JUNE 10, 1997

A SIMPLE PRACTICAL STEAM ENGINE WILL BE PRODUCED REDUCING THE WORLDS DEPENDENCE ON OIL. PERSONAL VEHICLES AND ENERGY PLANTS WILL BE THE FIRST TO CONVERT TO STEAM RESULTING IN A CLEANER ENVIRONMENT AND A MAJOR REALIGNMENT OF POLITICAL AND NATURAL WEALTH. THE COMING OF A NEW ICE AGE WILL BE AVERTED. ALSO THE CUBS WILL WIN A SERIES.

Address

Al OERTER
OLYMPIC GOLD MEDALIST
1956-60-64-68

© UNITED NATIONS

A simple practical steam engine will be produced reducing the world's dependence on oil. Personal vehicles and energy plants will be the first to convert to steam resulting in a cleaner environment and a major realignment of political and natural wealth. The coming of a new Ice Age will be averted. Also the Cubs will win a Series.

LOU GROZA

Birthplace:
Martin's Ferry, Ohio

Age at the
Millennium: 76

An NFL star from 1946 to 1967, Lou Groza was MVP numerous times in the 1950s and played in nine NFL title games. He later established a college scholarship fund. Groza was inducted into the Hall of Fame in 1974.

United Nations   Nations Unies
NEW YORK   GENÈVE

Address

    My message to all young people in the new millennium. "Take pride in yourself and all you do. Study hard, play hard and reap the benefits - family, religion and education. The fundamentals of life are similar to the fundamentals of sports. Good morals are timeless. Good luck always- all ways."

Lou Groza
"The Toe"
Berea, Ohio
7-24-97

©
UNITED
NATIONS

263   A basketball commentator on ESPN since 1979, Dick Vitale helped pioneer that experimental sports network. Vitale's energetic on-air superlatives earned him the 1989 Sports Personality of the Year Award from the American Sportscasters Association.

Birthplace:
Garfield, N.J.

Age at the Millennium: 55

DICK VITALE

United Nations   Nations Unies
NEW YORK   GENÈVE

Address

©
UNITED
NATIONS

My goal would be to see peace and love among all the people in the world. Also to see a cure found for cancer and AIDS! God Bless!

GREG LOUGANIS

Birthplace:
El Cajun, Calif.

Age at the Millennium: 40

A four-time Olympic gold medalist, Greg Louganis was the dominant American male diver at four Olympic games (1976–1988). Louganis has remained active in various social causes, including HIV prevention and domestic violence.

United Nations   Nations Unies
NEW YORK   GENÈVE

Hopes for a cure for HIV and cancer.
Also better understanding and tolerance to human diversity.

Address

©
UNITED
NATIONS

Hopes for a cure for HIV and cancer.
Also better understanding and tolerance to human diversity.

Photo by Victor Malafronte / Archive Photos

Italy's most famous athlete, Alberto Tomba's skiing successes include three gold and two silver Olympic medals in the slalom. Known as "La Bomba," Tomba is equally famous for his fast-track bachelor lifestyle, including racing Ferraris and appearing in motion pictures.

Birthplace:
Bologna, Italy

Age at the Millennium: 33

ALBERTO TOMBA

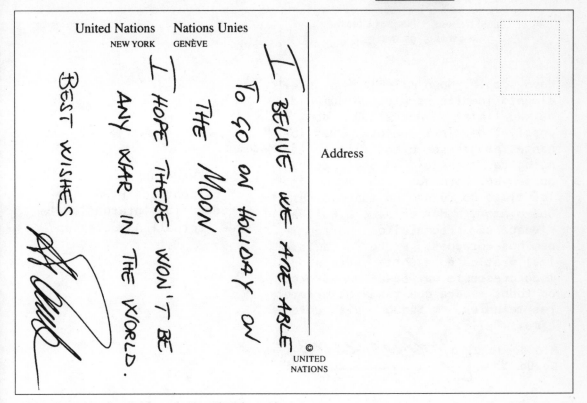

I believe we are able to go on holiday on the Moon. I hope there won't be any war in the world. Best Wishes.

DR. JOÃO HAVELANGE

Birthplace:
Rio de Janeiro, Brazil

Age at the Millennium: 84

As the leader of the international ruling soccer association, FIFA, João Havelange has presided over the most popular sport in the world since 1974. A Brazilian, Havelange's skillful administration has built a sports dynasty.

United Nations   Nations Unies
NEW YORK   GENÈVE

Novo século, Novo milênio - aconteci-mento inédito na vida da Humanidade. No limiar do Ano 2.000, só é possível desejar: Que os impressionantes progressos científicos e técnológicos conseguidos até agora, possam ser coroados com melhorias idênticas no futuro do mundo moral. Que o Amor, a Harmonia, e a Solidariedade sem preconceitos - predominem nos corações. E que a sadia e leal prática do esporte esteja de modo crescente na base do esforço de todos - para que tenhamos criaturas melhores, em mundo mais unido e mais feliz.

Rio de Janeiro,
06.08.1997

Address

JOÃO HAVELANGE
Presidente da FIFA
Fédération Internationale
de Football Association

© UNITED NATIONS

A new century, a new millennium—a new accomplishment in the life of mankind at the beginning of the year 2000, it is possible to wish for: That the remarkable scientific and technical progress obtained until now might be crowned with identical improvement in the future of the world's morals. May love, harmony and solidarity without prejudice dominate in our hearts. And may the honest and loyal practice of sport be the basis of everyone's effort to have better people in a united and greater world.

The only man to win the Kentucky Derby five times or twice be a Triple Crown winner, Eddie Arcaro retired in 1962 with 4,779 wins. Mr. Arcaro passed away in 1997 at age 80.

Birthplace:
Cincinnati, Ohio

Deceased 1997

EDDIE ARCARO

United Nations   Nations Unies
NEW YORK   GENÈVE

After surviving the present changes, the 21st Century will be the continuation of progress made now. Taking more responsibility will lead us in to "Universal Brotherhood" "All in One" One in All" "In the near future I see planetary traveling as easy, as going from Miami to New-York.

Eddie Arcaro

Address

June 1st 1997
Miami, Fla.

Eddie Arcaro

© UNITED NATIONS

After surviving the present changes, the 21st Century will be the continuation of progress made now. Taking more responsibility will lead us into "Universal Brotherhood," "All in One, One in All." In the near future I see planetary traveling as easy as going from Miami to New York.

PHIL RIZZUTO

Birthplace: New York, N.Y.

Age at the Millennium: 82

A Hall of Fame shortstop with the Yankees for fifteen years, Phil Rizzuto is best known for his subsequent sportscasting career. Rizzuto broadcast Yankees games for thirty-nine years, immortalizing his coverage with the trademark phrase, "Holy Cow!"

United Nations   Nations Unies
NEW YORK   GENÈVE

Address

UNITED NATIONS

The year 2000—"Holy Cow," just saying the year makes you want to be here for the great event and for a long time after—so many new ideas, inventions, more knowledge about our health and gains against the dread sickness of the big C and the heart—being an ex-big leaguer, and in the Hall of Fame, not only baseball, but all sports should be better than ever—I'm sure the young men and women will make us proud— the best of Health and Happiness to all.

Chapter 10

Predictions from the Authors

DAVID KRISTOF

Birthplace:
Chicago, Ill.

Age at the
Millennium: 34

Cofounder and director of the Millennium Committee of New York, David Kristof is an active volunteer with the Republican Party and at Saint Patrick's Cathedral. Kristof works for Lucent Technologies in New York City.

Predictions for the Next Millennium:

• The world will have one universal language, largely based on a phonetically simplified form of English. This language will not be created or initially endorsed by governments, but will develop from universities and media organizations. After some controversy, it will enjoy widespread acceptance from multi-national corporations and within a few generations be taught to schoolchildren worldwide. It will revolutionize global communications.

• Mankind will build settlements on the Moon and Mars, but their populations will be minute compared to the Earth's, due to the lack of a self-sufficient economic system or a desirable middle class lifestyle. These heavily dependent and artificial colonies will mainly be inhabited by an elite scientific and military class (much like in Antarctica today), living alongside a surreal hospitality industry built for wealthy tourists from Earth. Lunar and Martian environmental groups will protest ambitious plans to alter their terrain and atmospheres to suit the physical comforts of humans. Space travel will prompt a new appreciation for the goodness and fragility of the Earth.

• Public interest in space will be secondary to the interest in longevity. A growing portion of the world economy will be based on medically extending not just life-span but youthful appearances to those who can afford it. This will not only explode the populations of the developed countries but redefine social attitudes towards the elderly, which will include physically fit 300-year-olds. Society will develop a deeper sense of history and of respect for its past.

• A form of "Manifest Destiny" will be revived, with parts of Canada and the Americas (and even beyond) joining the United States (the only nation in the world formed on common ideals instead of common ethnic lineage). There will be many more stars in the American flag! And in the face of continued despair in the Third World, developing countries will one by one contract with American and other Western nations' institutions to acquire "pre-built" systems of social structures - including legal, electoral, economic, educational, health care and communications systems. It will be the "assembly-line" version of globalized democracy and bring peace, prosperity and dignity to billions of lives.

• An increasingly violent continuation of wars and terrorism into the new millennium will eventually prompt us to evolve our everyday thinking and conduct. We will finally acknowledge that the natural human impulse to justify destructiveness must be disciplined, and that developing our positive energies is not only our responsibility but is our evolution. This acknowledgment will be the most meaningful development of the next millennium.

David Kristof

New York City, 1998

DAVID KRISTOF

Photo by Larry Lettera

Cofounder and director of the Millennium Committee of New York, Todd W. Nickerson lives with his wife and two sons in New Jersey. An MBA graduate from Fairleigh Dickinson University, Nickerson is employed with Lucent Technologies.

Birthplace:
Wareham, Mass.

Age at the Millennium: 32

TODD W. NICKERSON

I predict that with the Third Millennium, man will experience a 'renaissance,' a reevaluation of its purpose and of its effect on the other inhabitants of this beautiful world of ours (which by the way not only includes humans but also plants and animals). This introspective voyage will be spurred by a long overdue development of a sense of 'personal responsibility' among men and women of all colors and creeds. And with this newfound sense of responsibility mankind will wonder how we survived the Second Millennium.

I believe in a few hundred years mankind will look back at today's world and wonder how we could stand by and watch our environment destroyed. We'll marvel at the wars we've raged upon ourselves - Civil Wars is what they'll be regarded as in another thousand years. This is of course not to say we won't be warring with someone else in the Universe!

I also believe by 2050 a fool-proof means of birth control will be developed greatly reducing the strain of overpopulation and the tragedy of unwanted and unloved children. We'll colonize the Moon, Mars and continue on to explore the Universe; searching, exploring and seeking understanding, just as we have for thousands of years.

Todd W. Nickerson
New York, NY
March 1, 1998

Index